THE UNTOLD STORY
OF THE CLEMENT-WITCHER FEUD

Beverly Merritt

DEDICATION

This book is dedicated to the Glory of God
and in honor of my good friend, Dorothy Hodges, Franklin County Librarian,
for her hard work and dedication to Franklin County, Virginia genealogy..

TABLE OF CONTENTS

INTRODUCTION

More of the Story

The Clement-Witcher Feud is a story that endures to this day, divorce, murder and mayhem between two prominent families has survived for more 150 years.   A beautiful young woman married only a couple years wanted relief from a supposedly abusive husband. When it ended her husband and two of his brothers lay dead after a bloody encounter at Washington Dickinson's Store, her grandfather, brother and other family members accused of murder,

The story seems to hang on a statement by one party at a deposition calling someone on the other side a liar. That may have been the catalyst for the bloody encounter but not the entire reason for such hatred on both sides. Records show that James R. Clement took his child, Lelia Maud Clement, away from his wife Victoria C. Clement as Victoria fled their home. He placed Lelia Maud with his brother's family and there is no clear record to show where Lelia Maud stayed after that. There is mention of a court suit over custody of the child. It would appear, after reading all the transcripts, that the custody of Lelia Maud was the basis for this feud.

There is a book in the Franklin County Library that contains a typed version of the depositions taken in this case. The identity of the typist is not known and the information appears to have been taken from Dr. George W. Clement's book published in 1860. This typed version was never completed, several paragraphs were left off the last page and I always wondered about the last bit of information and set out to find it. There is a complete copy of Dr. Clement's original book in the Bassett Historical Center.

Vincent A. Witcher was indeed a prominent and powerful man in the Commonwealth of Virginia. Dr. George W. Clement, father of the men who died, was also well-to-do and as one newspaper account states: "They frequently visited one another, counseled together, and interchanged all the ordinary transactions of life", *Petersburg Express.*

Not all the court documents survived to be microfilmed by the Library of Virginia but those that did contain more information than found in other accounts, Pittsylvania County documents are also found in that file. Brief descriptions of the proceedings are found in the Chancery Court Order Books in Franklin County but no actual testimony. The Chancery records show that the bodies were examined by a coroner and an inquest held but no report could be found.

Unfortunately the Franklin County newspapers for this time period were lost in a fire. However, the *Petersburg Express,* Petersburg, Virginia provided a colorful, if at times somewhat inaccurate, picture of the people and events.

The most complete source for this information is the transcribed record, "*THE EVIDENCE IN THE CASE OF THE COMMONWEALTH VERSUS VINCENT WITCHER, ADDISON WITCHER SAMUEL SWANSON, JOHN A. SMITH AND VINCENT O. SMITH".* published June 14, 1860 by Dr. George W. Clement, father of the three brothers who died that day.

A Speedy Trial

Documents show that Court was held between sunrise and sunset. September 22nd, 1859 "The further taking of depositions is adjourned till to-morrow morning half past six *oclock",* court actually did not commence that day until "forty minutes past seven o"clock". Other days began at various times. The murder trial was not delayed, depositions were started on February 29, 1860 at the house of Andrew S. Brooks.

We do not know the date Captain Witcher and John Anthony Smith were arrested, they surrendered to the Sheriff about March 15, 1860; a not guilty plea was entered March 19, 1860. There is no record of the arrest of the other three accused, they were all accused of murder and acquitted May 16, 1860. The records show Captain Witcher and John A. Smith were denied bail and spent the intervening time in jail.

Punctuation, Spelling and Grammar

I wonder how the Clerk recorded the questions and answers posed during the depositions and trial, he may have taken notes in shorthand; it is easy to see by the handwriting that more than one Clerk recorded these proceedings.

The terms deposition and testimony appear to have been used interchangeably. The divorce suit was not brought before a Judge, these were only preliminary proceedings.

Some records of the depositions were written on lined paper but most of the pages were not lined. Questions on a few pages appear to have been written by one person and the answers added by another. Rules for spelling, punctuation and grammar were not as important as the information being recorded. If the Clerk had to write down each and every word he had to write very quickly and could not stop to consider commas, etc. Any word appearing in this book in italics indicates a word as it appears on the document. Punctuation marks were added to Dr. Clement"s book, they were not generally used in the original documents.

Commas and periods were sometimes impossible to distinguish and periods seldom used. For that reason there are no periods at the end of most sentences; question marks were not used at all.

If a word or phrase appears in parenthesis shaped (-), that is an original quote. If they parenthesis are shaped {-} the notation is from the author of this volume. Proper use of grammar does not necessarily reflect the intelligence, education or social status of a person and colloquialisms are spread all through these pages.

CONTEMPORARY NEWSPAPER ACCOUNTS

Petersburg Express, Petersburg, Virginia, February 26, 1860

"It appears that some years since, a granddaughter of the venerable and talented Vincent Witcher, Esq. of Pittsylvania county, married a gentleman from the adjoining county of Henry, whose name was *Clemmens*. His Christian name we have been unable to ascertain. The maiden name of Mr. Witcher''s grand-daughter was Smith. The parties lived happily together until about eighteen months since, when, upon the most unfounded suspicions, as we have been informed, Mr. *Clemmens* desired a separation from his wife, and immediately instituted proceedings for a divorce, at the same time *inpeaching* her honor as the grounds for his course.

Last Saturday was set apart for the taking of depositions, and the parties met at a magisterial precinct in Henry county. Mr. Witcher appeared to defend the suit and protect the honor of his grand-daughter. The taking of the depositions progressed, and, after the plaintiff had finished with a witness, Mr. Witcher asked a question, which greatly exasperated the husband, Mr. *Clemmens*. He immediately arose, drawing a pistol at the same time, and fired at Mr. Witcher. Mr. Witcher, it seems, also quickly rose, and drew a pistol from his pocket, and as the ball of his antagonist grazed around the abdomen, he fired, striking *Clemmens* in the forehead and killing him instantly.

A nephew of Mr. Witcher, and a Mr. Smith, brother of Mrs. *Clemmens*, hearing the firing, rushed into the room. A brother of Mr. *Clemmens*, who had also been attracted by the pistol-reports, fired at a nephew of Mr. Witcher, the ball taking effect, and producing, it is feared, a fatal wound. Upon seeing his nephew shot, Mr. Vincent Witcher again fired, striking *Clemmens* No. 2 and killing him instantly.

At this stage of the sanguinary affair, Mr. Smith, a brother of Mrs. *Clemmens*, drew a bowie-knife, but had scarcely unsheathed the blade when he was fired upon by a second brother of *Clemmens*, the ball taking effect in the shoulder, and producing a painful wound. Infuriated by his wound, Mr. Smith rushed upon his antagonist, and with one powerful thrust of the knife completely disemboweled *Clemmens* No. 3, the unfortunate man falling dead on the spot.

Three of the parties died, and the other three all wounded, the horrible tragedy here ended.

Vincent Witcher, Esq., the chief actor in this truly terrible affair, is widely known throughout Virginia. He served for many years in the lower House of the Legislature and subsequently represented his district in the State Senate with signal ability. He is a prominent member of the Whig party, and his name has been repeatedly mentioned in connection with the office of Governor of the Commonwealth. He succeeded Whitmell P. Tunstall, upon the death of that gentleman, as President of the Richmond & Danville Railroad. After two years'' service, he resigned the presidency of the road, and has since been engaged in the practice of his profession, - that of a lawyer.

Our informant states that throughout this painful suit, which Mr. Witcher believes to have been instituted against his grand-daughter, he has acted with great forbearance, and the part he has been compelled finally to act will be with none a source of deeper regret than himself."

Petersburg Register, Petersburg, Virginia, February 27, 1860

"As we anticipated, the hurried account we gave yesterday of the killing of the three brothers Clement - and not Clemmens, as stated by us - contained a few errors, regarding locality and names, which we hasten to correct. This we are enabled to do through the kindness of a gentleman now residing in our midst, who once lived in the section of country where the horrible tragedy was enacted., and is intimately acquainted with all the parties who participated in this most deplorable and truly bloody affair.

The feud existing between the Witcher and the Clement families is of long duration - some twelve months or more - and grew out of the marriage of Mr. James Clement, who is the youngest of five brothers, with Miss Victoria Smith, and a grand-daughter of the late Dr. Albert Smith and a grand-daughter of Vincent Witcher, Esq. The parties are all wealthy, and occupy a high social position in the respective counties which they represent, the Clements belonging to Franklin and the Witchers to Pittsylvania county.

The marriage between Mr. James Clement and Miss Victoria Smith was solemnized about two years ago last fall, and the nuptials were celebrated with great *éclat,* a brilliant party being given in honor of the event, which was attended by the *elite* of the two counties, who flocked in large numbers, by invitation, from all parts of that section, to do honor to the joyous occasion. For several months the wedded pair lived together with naught but the most unalloyed happiness shining on the rosy pathway of their early matrimonial career. At length the "green-eyed" monster, jealousy, reared his horrid front in the household of the happy couple, and ultimately placed such restrictions upon the young and confiding wife as to render her very existence a burden too intolerable o be borne.

She finally resolved to leave the roof of her husband, and removed to the residence of her mother, Mrs Dr. Albert Smith, in the county of Pittsylvania, where she now resided, and by the advice of her friends, during the fall of 1859, instituted suit against her husband for divorce. Soon after the institution of the suit, the parties met at Sandy Level, Pittsylvania county, for the purpose of taking depositions. Here a charge was made by the husband, Mr. James Clement, which involved alike the honor of his wife and that of Mr. William P. Gilbert, a young gentleman present, which was resented by Mr. Gilbert on the spot. Pistols were drawn, and nine shots exchanged, five of which took effect, injuring Mr. Gilbert and his brother, as well as two of the Messrs. Clement, but none of them seriously.

This serious affray, of course, greatly increased the ill feeling which had been engendered between the parties; and the matter finally became so much talked of that most of the citizens of the two counties were involved in the difficulty, each party having his warm and zealous adherents.

Added to other causes which had so estranged the two families, some time since Mr. James Clement, the husband, by some means obtained possession of a sprightly child, the only issue of the marriage, and placed it with his own relatives. The grand-father, Captain Witcher, and a large party of friends, deeming this act an outrage, and believing that the mother was the proper custodian of the offspring, by due process of law recovered the infant and restored it to its maternal parent.

Last Saturday, the 25th instant, as stated yesterday, the parties all met a a locality in Franklin county (some say *Brooks's* and others Dickinson"s store,) to take further depositions to be used in the suit now pending for divorce. A question proposed by Captain Witcher so exasperated Mr. James Clement, the defendant in the suit, that he resorted to the use of his pistol for an answer, but fired too quickly to make sure of his aim. Captain Witcher returned the fire, and killed the husband of his grand-daughter on the spot, the *bll* striking in the forehead. Ralph Clement, rushing to his brother"s aid shared the same fate, from the discharge of a pistol in the same hands which had sped the messenger of death with such unerring certainty to the brain of his brother James. Johnson Clement, another brother, fired at Mr. John Archer Smith, a grandson of Mr. Witcher, who was present, and brother to Mrs. Victoria Clement, severely wounding him in the shoulder. The wounded man then rushed upon Johnson Clement with a bowie- knife, and made a fatal thrust into his bowels, the unfortunate victim falling dead on the spot. The other party to the affray, engaged by the Witcher side, was a Mr. Samuel Swanson, Jr., also a devoted grandson of Mr. Witcher. Mr. Swanson was wounded but will recover. Mr. Smith, the brother of Mrs. Clement, it is thought, will die of the severe wound received in the shoulder.

Mr. James Clement was about twenty-eight years of age, and the youngest of five brothers. He was a farmer by occupation. His brother Ralph was a lawyer, and *Johnson*, the other brother killed, was, like James, also a farmer. Two other brothers emigrated West several years ago. The father of the unfortunate men who have thus met such violent deaths is Dr. George Clement, a very wealthy and prosperous farmer. He formerly resided in Franklin county, but has recently removed to Pittsylvania.

Mrs. Victoria Clement (formerly Miss Victoria Smith) is said to be a lady of about twenty-one years of age, possesses extraordinary personal beauty, and is highly accomplished. She is a daughter of the late Dr. Albert Smith, who died leaving a large estate and five children, two sons and three daughters. His widow still survived, with whom Mrs. Victoria Clement has resided since she left the house of her husband.

Captain Vincent Witcher is, perhaps, as widely known in Virginia as any man within the limits of the Commonwealth. For twenty-one consecutive years, in the popular branch as well as in the Senate of our State legislature he had played no unimportant part. His speeches in the Legislature always commanded the undivided attention of that body, and were characterized by a force of logic and power of reasoning that rendered them *wellnigh* irresistible.

5

We understand that up to the time of the difficulties growing out of the unfortunate marriage between the two families, Dr. Clement and Vincent Witcher, Esq., were what may be termed bosom-friends. They frequently visited one another, counseled together, and interchanged all the ordinary transactions of life.

The following quotes appear in the transcript of a speech, "A Thorough Masonic Investigation", given by Frater Paul E. Sutherland, June 15, 1974 at the annual Convention of Virginia College SRICF. Unfortunately he did not give his sources for these newspapers:

"One had his throat cut from ear to ear, another had his body severed in twain and the third almost had his heart cut out to be exposed {Ralph Clement}."

" „Ralph Clement rose and said, "If any person says I brought her here under my care and control, it is a lie". Some witnesses claimed there was even stronger language. „There was a silence, at least long enough for Colonel Carter to shake his head at Ralph, then get almost out of the room.

Captain Witcher rose from his chair and said, „Make your charge more definite, it you like!

There was a general movement from the room"s two doors. The spectators knew that according to the code of the day a fight probably would ensue. Ralph Clement had „given the lie" to Captain Witcher and the elderly gentle-man had picked up the challenge. Ralph was noted for fighting, not for for backing down"."

"… the dispute finally ended in James Clement drawing a revolver from his pocket, which he discharged several times at Captain W., but without effect, whereupon the latter drew his revolver and fired upon Clement, the ball taking effect and killing him instantly.

The other two brothers of C. then fired at Witcher, but neither of them struck him. Witcher, in the meantime, discharged the remaining balls in his pistol, and succeeded in fatally wounding both of the Clements; … each severely wounded.

Samuel Swanson, the son-in-law of Captain Witcher, used his cane, his only weapon. When the shooting started, he saw James was about to fire on Captain Witcher. He struck James Witcher across the arm, thus diverted the ball intended for the Captain in time. The ball went across his shoulder. This gave Witcher the needed time to return his fire at James. His shot was not wasted. The ball struck James squarely between the eyes, killing him instantly. William rushed to the side of his dead brother and at the same time commenced firing at Captain Witcher. Again, Samuel Swanson with his cane struck William on the arm holding the gun, thus diverting the shot. The ball this time went between Captain Witcher"s legs. Others said it was Ralph who rushed to the side of James and was shot."

The Lorain Eagle, March 15, 1860

"The *Lynchburg Republican* of Wednesday says that Mr. Vincent Witcher and his grandson (John Anthony Smith) surrendered themselves to the authorities and were promptly acquitted on the grounds of self-defense."

The *North Carolina Standard,* Wednesday, March 21, 1860

"Vincent Witcher, Esq. Committed – Bail Refused – It is stated that the examination of Vincent Witcher, Esq. for the killing of the three brothers, James, Ralph and Johnson {sic} Clement, at Dickenson"s store {sic}, Franklin County, on Saturday, the 25th of February, has resulted in his committal to jail for trial Bail was asked, but refused. Mr. John Anthony Smith, a grandson, and Mr. (William) Addison Witcher, son of Mr. Vincent Witcher, who were likewise implicated, have been sent on for trial before an Examining Court, which is to be held on Monday, Next, the 26th instant."

"Raleigh Standard", March 28, 1860

"Acquittal of Captain Vincent Witcher and Others
Lynchburg, Va. – March 25 – Capt. Vincent Witcher, Addison Witcher, J.A. Smith and Sam'l Swanson tried for killing the Messrs. Clements in Franklin County, Va., were acquitted Friday evening last."

LIVES TOUCHED AND FAMILY RELATIONSHIPS

Addison Witcher was a son of Vincent A. Witcher

Colonel Madison Carter was married to a sister of the Clements

Dr. George W. Clement, 1786-1867, was the father of James R., Ralph A., Johnston and William Clement, as well as 6 other children

James Reid Clement was a son of Dr. George W. Clement

Johnston Clement was s son of Dr. George W. Clement

John Anthony Smith was a brother of Victoria C. Clement and son of Alfred G. Smith and Mary Ann Witcher Smith, grandson of Vincent A. Witcher; he was about 20 years of age when he served as Victoria"s "next friend" in the divorce suit

Lelia Maud Clement, born March 1, 1859, was the daughter of James R. Clement and Victoria C. Clement

Mary Ann Witcher Smith was a daughter of Vincent A. Witcher

Ralph A. Clement was a son of George W. Clement

Samuel Southard Berger was named in a deposition as possibly having been engaged to Victoria C. Clement prior to her marriage with James R. Clement

Samuel Swanson was Vincent A. Witcher"s son-in-law

Shirwood {S.Y.} Shelton was Overseer for Johnston Clement and lived in Johnston"s house

Silas {Sile} Dudley was married to Victoria C. Clement"s sister

Victoria C. {Smith} Clement was a daughter of Alfred G. Smith and Mary Ann Witcher Smith, grand-daughter of Vincent A. Witcher; born September 2, 1838 in Pittsylvania County, died August 27, 1899 at Timmonsville, Florence County, South Carolina, buried in the Byrd Cemetery; married Samuel Southard Berger and is possibly the mother of Jacob William Berger {1872-1929}

Vincent A. Witcher, born @1786 was not a young man in February of 1860 and the time he spent in jail awaiting and during the trial must have been difficult for him. An attorney, Capt. Witcher had served in the Virginia House of Delegates and Senate between 1823 and 1854. He was the namesake and a member of the Vincent A. Witcher Masonic Lodge, chartered 12-15-1852. {Note: It was very rare for a lodge to bear the name of a living namesake} In 1860 the Lodge had a membership of 39, including James R. Clement and his brother Ralph A. Clement, their deaths were recorded in the Lodge records.

Historian Marshall Wingfield tells in his book "An Old Virginia Court" of a letter he received from the Secretary of the Grand Lodge of Virginia, James N. Hillman:

"I find no reference to him subsequent to 1860 in the list of expulsions, suspensions or membership. Evidently something happened to him, but it is not reported in the minutes from that lodge. The name of Vincent A. Witcher, who shed the blood of his brother Masons, has not been perpetuated by Masonry".

No returns for this Lodge were filed for the years 1860 thru 1866 but these were the War years and this may have had nothing to do with Capt. Witcher. The Vincent A. Witcher Lodge lost its charter in 1885 because no reports were filed for more than three years and was marked extinct in 1886. This failure would not have had anything to do with Capt. Witcher or this case.

Vincent Oliver Smith was a brother of Victoria C. Clement and son of Alfred G. Smith and Mary Ann Witcher Smith, grandson of Vincent A. Witcher

William Clement was a son of Dr. George W. Clement

TIMELINE

05-13-1858 - James R. Clement and Victoria C. Smith were married

05-16-1858 - They attended a party at Vincent A. Witcher''s house and James appeared unhappy with Victoria's conduct

03-01-1859 - James and Victoria''s daughter Lelia Maud was born, a mere 10 months after the marriage

08-24-1859 - Victoria fled her home & went to Johnston Clement''s house where his Overseer S.Y. Shelton lived

08-30-1859 - Victoria filed a Bill of Complaint {for divorce} in Pittsylvania County

08-30-1859 - Miscellaneous Document #1 & #2

08-31-1859 - A Court Order for support for Victoria and daughter Maud was issued by the Court in Pittsylvania County

09-01-1859 - Miscellaneous Document #3

09-05-1859 - Miscellaneous Document #4

09-13-1859 - Depositions started at Sandy Level, Pittsylvania County

09-15-1859 - William P. Gilbert was to resume deposition but before 9 am 9 shots were fired, 5 took effect: James R. Clement and brother Johnston were wounded, both bed-ridden for some time, William P. Gilbert and brother {unnamed} were also injured

09-20-1859 - James R. Clement wrote his will leaving everything to daughter Lelia Maud

09-21-1859 - S.Y. Shelton''s deposition at Dickinson''s Store

09-22-1859 - Ralph A. Clement filed an Exception to the depositions being taken if James could not be there {James had been shot at Sandy Level a week previous}

09-22 and 27-1859 - S.Y. Shelton''s deposition

10-20-1859 - James R. Clement filed his answer to the divorce complaint; accusing Victoria of infidelity with William P. Gilbert

Late 1859 - William C. Clement, attorney, returned from Colorado

{During the winter both sides took target practice and made sure the other side knew about it}

Depositions at Washington Dickinson''s Store

02-21-1860 - George Sampson deposition

02-24-1860 - Edney Shelton deposition

02-25-1860 - James R. Clement, Ralph A. Clement and William Clement were killed;

02-27-1860 - Coroner''s Inquest was held but no records were found

02-29-1860 - Depositions began for murder trial of Vincent A. Witcher, Addison Witcher, John A. Smith, Samuel Swanson and Vincent O. Smith

@03-15-1860 - Vincent A. Witcher and John A. Smith surrendered to Sheriff

03-23-1860 - Verdict of Not Guilty

06-14-1860 - Dr. George W. Clement published transcripts *"THE EVIDENCE IN THE CASE OF THE COMMONWEALTH VERSUS VINCENT WITCHER, ADDISON WITCHER, SAMUEL SWANSON, JOHN A. SMITH AND VINCENT O. SMITH"*

Date not known - Victoria C. Smith Clement married Samuel Southard Berger

IN THEIR OWN WORDS

The following excerpts are taken from depositions, testimony and other documents touching the main events of this case. It may be easier to understand the events when taken as a whole than bits and pieces spread among the statements in the testimonies. The entire testimony of individual witnesses, as recorded and available, can be found later in this volume.

ATTORNEYS

"Ralph Clement was managing for the defendant {his brother James R. Clement} and a gentleman by the name of Dabney a part of the time during Thursday and part of Friday. What time of day Dabney left on Friday I do not recollect. The balance of the time, Addison Witcher {son of Vincent A. Witcher} for the plaintiff, to the best of my recollection, during the time I was present"

Jacob Mackenhamer

Captain Vincent A. Witcher also acted as attorney for Victoria C. Clement and her brother John A. Smith acted as her next friend in Court.

VICTORIA C. CLEMENT'S BILL OF COMPLAINT

To the Hon. George H. Gilmer, Judge of the Circuit Court of the County of Franklin - Humbly complaining *shews* unto your Honor your Oratrix Victoria C. Clement formerly Victoria Smith a married woman who sues by her next friend John Anthony Smith, that on the 13th day of May, 1858

She intermarried with James Clement. Your Oratrix is now in her twenty-second year.

A few days after said marriage the said James R Clement commenced towards her a system of persecution & cruelty. About the 3rd day after the marriage they came on a visit to her Grandfather's, where they met many of their relations & many of the young persons of the neighborhood. A dance was commenced with the permission & sanction of her Grandfather & your Oratrix joined in it. The said James Clement immediately went off to another room sullen & angry, & reproached her for joining in the dance & for conversing with the young persons present, telling her that as she was then a married woman she should not converse with other men or join in any gaiety. He did not pretend that time, nor was there, any indecorous frivolity in her conduct, but she was censored solely on the ground that she should thenceforth take no part in the amusements of young persons or conversation with young men.

A few days after they went to the house of said Clement & established themselves in housekeeping. For two or three months after this they lived in comparative quiet & peace, your Oratrix during this time staying closely at home attending to her household duties, and endeavoring in every way to make his house pleasant to her husband, and to accommodate herself to his views of propriety. Occasionally, during this period, after visits from their neighbors during which nothing more than the common courtesies of friendly intercourse were exchanged, he would become moody, sulky & fretful & would intimate to her by distant insinuations that she ought not to converse with other men.

He always accompanied her to church & generally took his seat by her and *sidulously* avoided leaving her for a moment. They generally went in a buggy, & if any male acquaintance rode to the side of the buggy & entered into conversation, he would become sullen & angry. She often asked him what the matter was or asked him to explain the cause of his anger, & he would evade the question & the subject was generally dropped. After two or three months had passed he became more violent. He would often then tell her positively that she should not converse with other men. That he suspected her fidelity to him. She ascertained that she was *enciente* and he would often with oaths declare to her that the child with which she was pregnant was not his. He had in the house a bowie-knife, a Colt"s pistol and a sword cane. He would often *mould* bullets, load his pistol before her & declare that he meant to shoot *some one* whose name he would not give. About five months after the marriage three young men visited at the house, who *staid* all night and slept in the rooms on the second floor your Oratrix & her said husband slept on the first floor in the same room & bed. The next morning he came to her & told her that one of the outer doors of the house was found open when he rose she thought nothing of the circumstances as the doors hooks were old & worn & were frequently opened by the wind. When the young men came down to breakfast, he asked one of them, Wm. P. Gilbert, in an angry tone, whether he had come down during the night. Gilbert denied that he had. After the young men left he accused your Oratrix of incontinence with Gilbert. Said that Gilbert knew all about the open door & that she did too. After this he would lock all the doors of the house at night would prepare his weapons and generally take his pistol & bowie-knife in bed with him, would compel her to get into bed & then before retiring would place chairs in the passage & around the bed so that any one moving in the room would move against them. He would often get up at the slightest noise made by the wind at the doors or windows & peep from the windows or creep around the house. This conduct was continued until the 1st of March 1859 when your Oratrix was delivered on a female child which was named Lelia Maud. Your Oratrix after her delivery was very ill & continued so for some weeks. During her illness her said husband whenever he was alone with her would reproach, insult and curse her. When any one was present he would endeavor to appear Kind & affectionate. During her illness he even became jealous of the physician attending her & reproached her & because the physician in examining her placed his hand on her breast. After her recovery he became still more unkind. He often told her that she should be entirely in subjection that she should not converse with any other young man and that if she did so she should leave his house. He would be apparently kind & affectionate to her before others, but as soon as again alone he would renew his abuse and slanderous charges. He continued to lock all the doors at night, to lay chairs about the bed & in the passage, & on one occasion tied a string from the door to the bed so as to trip up *any one* who might pass. On one occasion she went with him to preaching and the place being crowded, she with her Mother & other ladies took seat on a bench next to those occupied by the gentlemen of the Congregation. He reproached her for this as vulgar & indecent & told her that it was evidence of her guilt. On another occasion he went with her to church and insisted on going with her to the seats occupied exclusively by the ladies, where he sat by her during the services. She retired during the services to nurses her infant, and he insisted on accompanying her & did so, as he said to watch her. On returning home he told her that he had an eye-witness to the fact that she had that day given Gilbert the wink "That he then had proof of the fact of her unfaithfulness".

On the 24th of August, 1859, before she rose from her bed, he commenced abusing, cursing and insulting her, and accusing her of adultery. She gave no answer, determined to say nothing to him. This seemed to make him more violent. Finding that she would not reply he took a negro boy which had been advanced her by her mother & who was about six years old, stripped him naked and lashed him unmercifully until the blood ran from him. At the time he stated to the boy that he *whipt* him because he had some time before cut down a plant of Tobacco. At dinner on the 24th of Aug the subject of his whipping the boy being mentioned, she told him that she knew that he *whipt* him only to distress her & that the fault complained of was only a pretense. He cursed her and answered that such was his object & that he would immediately after dinner tie the boy up before her & whip him until he died. As soon as she could do so she {told the} boy privately to run off to her Mother's about three miles off, which he did. On his looking for the boy after dinner & not finding him, she refused to tell him where the boy was. He then told her that as things had come to an extremity & "that she must now look out for the worst." He cussed her & seemed in such a rage with her that she became seriously alarmed for her safety. She then had a horse caught & was about leaving with her infant when he ran up to her, snatched the child from her and a servant who was about handing it to her and cursing her, ordered her to leave. She immediately rode off to her mother's. On the same evening he rode up to her *Mothers* & asked for her. Her Mother went to the door & asked him to come in, but this he refused to do & asked again for your Oratrix. Your Oratrix then went to the door & he asked her abruptly whether she was coming home - after some hesitation, moved with her longing to see her child & hoping even yet for some change for the better, she answered him that she would go home & in a short time. He then rode off. The next morning your Oratrix returned. But little passed between them during that day. He seemed sullen and thoughtful. About nine *oclock* on that night your Oratrix retired with her infant to bed. A short time after, she heard him give orders to the servants to have his horse fed & saddled & ready for him at a *moments* warning. He then ordered that a bucket of hot water should be brought in & placed in the chambers. He then called up two female negroes who slept in the house, accused them of conniving at the incontinence of your Oratrix & of assisting her in it & declared that he would make them confess or kill them. Your Oratrix rose from bed and put on part of her clothes & begged him to desist - he told her that when he was done with the negroes he would have a private conversation with her. He then made the negro men hold the said female negroes and *whipt* them most unmercifully. While he was whipping them, your Oratrix looked to the places where his weapons were generally kept & could not find them. She became satisfied that he intended to kill her & shrieked loudly for help. He then told her that he must have a private conversation with her which no one must hear. That she should confess her guilt. That he had had a man hired at $5 per week to watch her & that he had conclusive evidence against her & that she should confess. He then ordered all the negroes to go off from the house & not to come to it under any circumstances. That they must not regard any cries they might hear, but that if any one of them came near he would shoot him. She then told him that she believed he intended to kill her. He declared he would not. She then told him that she would talk with him, if he would let some of the negroes come into the house. He answered that their conversation must be private - that she should confess she told him that he was armed he denied that he was & told her that she must come in the other room and he would *shew* her his arms. She resisted - and she then told him she should see them & turned to go into the other room. As he turned, your Oratrix slipped aside and got away out of the house & ran off alone to the house of Mrs Shelton *abouat* one mile distant - The night was a dark one & thus your Oratrix was enabled to escape from him undiscovered - Shortly after arriving at *Sheltons*,

13

the said Clement came up on horseback & with oaths demanded to see her, repeating the charge of lewdness against her- Since the 25th Aug 1859, your Oratrix has been with her *Mothers* Long as this detail of oppression may seem it does not contain a full statement of the acts committed on your Oratrix since her marriage - Many others might be mentioned which show a settled purpose to render her life miserable.

Your Oratrix most expressly denies the truth of any charge made against her by her said husband. She denies that she has ever by word or look or action given even the slightest ground for suspicion of her unfaithfulness as a wife or want of virtue as a woman She denies that she has ever laid herself liable even to the charge of levity or imprudence. Her good name has ever been and is above suspicion. She challenges an investigation of her whole life, though the scrutiny be rigid to the verge of malignity –

She charges that she has striven in all things to be faithful to her marriage vows. She has borne with insult conumely and oppression & has been met with constant systematic persecuting cruelty and at the last, in fear for her life has been forced to fly from her husband. Her infant is *dependant* on its *Mothers* breast for support - It is in the custody of her husband, who has been applied to for it, & who refused to give it up -

By the will of her father Albert G. Smith, decd his estate worth about $20000.00 was left to his widow during her life or widowhood & at her death or marriage was to be divided equally among his five children of whom your Oratrix was one - Under the power to make advancements to the children her said mother has advanced your Oratrix about $600 in money and a boy slave named Silas worth $800.00 & stock & furniture *be* worth about $250.00 all of which has been received by the Said James R. Clement - The said James R Clement in other estate is worth about $8000 or $10,000 independently of a tract of land in his possession which is said to be a gift from his Father which is worth about $6,000.00. Your Oratrix charges that she has heard that he would renew his abuse & slanderous charges

That said James R. Clement now threatens and has expressed his intention to remove said infant child, Lelia, to the residence of his sister, the wife of Madison Carter, in Patrick or Floyd *county*, and to sell his estate in Virginia & to remove beyond the line of the State - She believes that he so intends.

Your Oratrix, desiring a divorce from her said Husband and the possession & custody of her said child is compelled to resort to this court for relief - In consideration whereof & your Oratrix being without remedy except in a Court of Chancery that the said James R. Clement is made a deft to this bill & compelled to answer its allegations particularly as though each were here repeated. That the possession & custody of his said child is ordered to be surrendered to him. That a divorce from bed & board between your Oratrix and the said James R. Clement be decreed. That by order of this Court the maintenance of your Oratrix the expenses of this suit and the personal liberty of your Oratrix be provided for & that such other & further relief be granted as equity & the case of your Oratrix requires. May it please etc

                    Victoria C. Clement Isaac

H. Carrington, Attorney for plaintiff

MISCELLANEOUS DOCUMENTS RE: SUPPORT AND CUSTODY {Note: the following documents, numbered 1 thru 6, have been inserted according to date}

MISCELLANEOUS DOCUMENT #1

Pittsylvania County SU

Before me a justice of the peace in & for said County This day personally appeared the within named Victoria C Clement & John A Smith & made oath that they verily believe the within Bill to be True - Sworn under my hand 30th Aug 1859

MISCELLANEOUS DOCUMENT #2

Pittsylvania County SU

Before me a justice of the peace in the County aforesaid this day personally appeared Vincent Witcher & N O Witcher & made oath that they verily believe the facts stated in the within Bill to be true - Sworn under my hand this 30 Aug 1859 -

    John D Hall J.P.

MISCELLANEOUS DOCUMENT #3

1st Sept 1839

That said James R. Clement now threatens & has expressed his intention to remove said infant child Lelia to the residence of his Sister the wife of Madison Carter in Patrick or Floyd County and to sell his estate in Virginia & to remove beyond the limits of the State - We believe that he so intends Your Oratrix desiring a divorce from her said Husband & the possession & custody of her said child is compelled to resort to the Court for relief - In consideration whereof & your Oratrix being without {can't read} except in a Court of Chancery that the said James R. Clement be made a deft to this bill & compelled to answer its allegations particularly as though each were her {can't read}. That a divorce from bed & board between your Oratrix & the said James R. Clement be decreed. That by the order of this Court the maintenance of your Oratrix the {can't read} of this suit & the personal of your Oratrix be provided for & that such other & further relief be granted as {can't read} & the case of {can't read} v Oratrix is given May it please etc

{several words were erased} of *possion* may seem it does not contain a full statement of the acts of cruelty committed on your Oratrix since her marriage - Many others might be mentioned which *shew* a settled purpose to render his life miserable -

Isaac H Carrington Atto for Pltff   *Fontain* C. Clement

MISCELLANEOUS DOCUMENT #4

Know all men by these presents that we James R Clement Ralph A Clement and Edward C Murphy are held and firmly bound unto John Anthony Smith as next friend of Victoria C. Clement in the sum of Ten thousand dollars, for the true payment of which we bind ourselves, our heirs & jointly and severally firmly by these presents. Sealed with our Seals and dated this 5th day of September 1859

The Condition of the above obligation is such that whereas the above named Victoria C. Clement who sues by John Anthony Smith her next friend, has instituted a suit for a divorce against the above bound James R Clement, and the Judge of the Circuit Court of Franklin conditioned to have his property real and personal forthcoming to answer any future order of the Court in the said cause, then the sheriff of said County is to take possession of the estate, real and personal of the said James R. Clement and to hold it until the further order of the said Court. Now therefore if the above bound James R Clement shall have his property both real and personal, forthcoming to answer any further order of the Court in the said cause, then the obligation to be void, else to remain in full force and virtue.

James R Clement R
A Clement
E C Murphy

`ANSWER OF JAMES R. CLEMENT

The answer of James R. Clement to a bill of complaint exhibited against him in the Circuit Court of Franklin County, by Victoria C. Clement, who sues by her next friend, John A. Smith.

This respondent, saving to himself the benefit of all proper exceptions to the said bill, and to the many errors, misstatements and false allegations therein contained, for answer thereunto, says:

That it is true that the complainant and himself were married on the 13th of May, 1858. But all the other matured allegations of the bill are a tissue of exaggerated and unfounded statements.

While it is true that the complainant and himself were at her grandfathers a few days after marriage that a dance was commenced that the complainant joined in it, and that before it was concluded respondent retired to another room – yet he did not do so in anger or with a view to mortify the complainant as alleged in the bill, but for the purpose of obtaining rest and sleep. Respondent is not a healthy man at best, and the loss of two previous night"s sleep had made him unwell and caused him to retire, and when he did so, he left the complainant and others engaged in what he regarded innocent amusement and he utterly denies that he reproached her for joining in the dance or for conversing with the young persons present on the occasion and he utterly denies the use of any cruelty or persecution on his part towards the complainant, but, on the contrary, he treated her with the utmost forbearance, although her conduct towards him was very often the most contemptuous and rude, and her conversation the most insulting she could use.

And he never used or offered to use any violence towards her nor ever gave her a cross-word but upon very few occasions, when he had been so harassed and excited by her abuse and reproaches of himself and his family, as to cause him, under the excitement of the moment, to reply to her as hereinafter stated, viz:

1st. The complainant had been in the habit of throwing up to and taunting respondent with every disagreeable occurrence that ever took place among his friends with the addition of other things wholly untrue and unmerited. His brothers and sisters were subjects of her constant abuse even his gray-headed father did not escape, but was very often the subject of her severest invectives. Upon one occasion when she was thus railing out upon and abusing his relatives in the most vehement manner, your respondent"s patience being completed exhausted, had replied to her by asking, "if she was not ashamed to make such false and scandalous charges against his friends" and added, "even in her charges were true, had she ever considered how little right she had to speak of them to his *perdjudice,* for where continued your respondent, "are your own relations" going on to mention several of them, including her mother and father. Your respondent does not know that he was right in thus making reproachful allusions to her relations, and regretted it afterwards. But at the time, he regarded it as the only means of freeing himself from her annoying and constant abuse of his nearest and dearest relations.

2nd. On another occasion, the complainant, without any just cause, struck your respondent a blow in anger, when he told her "she must do it no more." Repeating the offence a third time, respondent then told her, "if she did {it} again he would certainly box her jaws." She never did repeat it afterwards, and respondent never laid his hands on her in anger. And these your respondent avers, spoken under the circumstances aforesaid, were the only cross words he ever spoke to the complainant.

Your respondent is amazed at complainant"s charge that she remained quietly at home after her marriage trying to accommodate herself to her notions of propriety. So far from this being true, she did not remain at home more than half of her time. And so far from trying to accommodate herself to your respondent"s notions of propriety, her general course of conduct towards him was *dictatorious*, contemptuous and insulting in the extreme, especially in private. For some cause, unknown to him, she seemed to cherish the utmost aversion to your respondent, and he was unable to please her in any respect. All of his advances toward familiarity and fondness were repelled with apparent scorn, and one-half of her time she did not occupy the same bed-chamber much less the same bed with your respondent.

Your respondent denies that he ever said that the complainant"s infant daughter was not his child. He believes is his child, although he is informed that the complainant is in the habit of getting angry when told her child favored respondent.   It is true the complainant during her pregnancy said peculiarly, "suppose the child"s eyes are black" to which respondent replied laughing, and in the same peculiar spirit, "if they are I will now own it." But he little thought that this *disreserved* confidence and pleasantry of a marriage bed-chamber, merely had for the amusement of each other, would form the basis of so grand a charge against him.

It is wholly untrue that respondent put any restraint on the complainant as to her conversing with or keeping the company of other men, old or young, except that he did, for what he considered good and sufficient reasons, request her to desist from all conversations or communications with the said Wm. P. Gilbert. So far from this being true the complainant was remarkable for her gayety and life both at home and abroad, and not only entirely disregarded your respondent"s request in regard to said Gilbert but was in the constant habit of receiving attentions from other unmarried men, as to which your respondent offered no objections or remonstrance.

But a few days before her final rupture with respondent, she took a young man by the hand in respondent"s presence, led him near the railings of an upper porch and said that she was going to throw him over or make him take "the lover"s leap" and on taking leave the same young man attempted to kiss her in respondent"s presence. Respondent does not believe the young man had any evil design and simply mentions the circumstance to show that the complainant was not under the restraint she pretends to have been in her said bill. While respondent is free to say that

17

he did not approve such conduct, yet he did not reprove complainant for it, because experience had taught him it would do no good and would be followed by a tirade of abuse. And so far from her heeding your respondent"s request as to said Gilbert or accommodating her "conduct to your respondent"s notions of propriety", she not only did not desist from conversing with him but was in the habit of being waited on by him at church, and when respondent preferred his aforesaid request to her in relation to her intercourse with the said Gilbert she became furiously mad and violent in her language to your respondent.

Your respondent denies that his conduct towards the complainant was different in private from what it was in public. But on the contrary he avers it was his constant effort to please her and to be kind and conciliatory towards her.
It is true that respondent generally accompanied the complainant to church, and did on one or two occasions take a seat by her on the gentlemen"s seats, the seats for the ladies having been previously filled. He did not on but one other occasion and then only for a few moments seat himself by her at church nor did he then do it to watch her nor did he ever tell complainant that he would watch her. Her statements in this regard are erroneous. Your respondent denies that he ever complained to the complainant of her conduct towards, or the conduct or deportment of other persons towards her except in the case of Gilbert and especially of her attending physician on the contrary, the best understanding existed between the said physician and himself, and he had no cause to complain of the physician in any respect.

Your respondent denies that he ever put any restraint upon the complainant in respect to going anywhere or conversing with any person she pleased, except the said Gilbert, and even this he did in as kind and conciliatory a manner as the case would admit of.

As to the opening of the door, mentioned in the complainant"s bill, it is true that upon the occasion mentioned in the bill, when the young men *staid* all night at complainant"s house, he found the door of the house open next morning, and supposing that some of them might have gone out during the night and left it open on returning, he enquired of one of them in the morning but whether of Gilbert or some other he does not recollect if he had gone out during the night, and received for answer that he had not. But he denies that he did so in an angry manner indeed he thought but little of the circumstances at that time, and it made no impression on his mind. Before this a certain double door of respondent"s house began to be opened during the night in rather a mysterious manner, which he at first supposed might be the effect of the wind or the fault of an old lock. Your respondent was then particular in fastening it so as to leave no doubt about how it was opened. Still it continued occasionally to be opened during night time. Surprised at this, respondent fastened the bolt in the thimble of the door so as to make it impossible for *any one* to open it except on the inside. After this was done the door was again opened, but only one wing of it, the bolt having been so fastened in the thimble as to render it difficult to be opened. This opening of the door occasionally had continued for several weeks, during which time the complainant and respondent were several times absent on visits. And upon their return from abroad she would go into the house first and to another door and proclaim it to have been broken open. This happened several times and the complainant caused respondent to chastise his servants for it. Respondent then made a new bolt for this door. Shortly after this, when complainant and respondent returned home from a visit whilst she went into the house respondent was busied about the vehicle in which they had rode, and on his going into the house after her, he distinctly saw deliberately break the bolt from the door and heard it fall on the floor, when she immediately cried out that the house had been broken open and called your respondent"s attention to it. And he then began to suspect her of knowing something about the opening of the doors. Respondent then fastened the door again, after which the double door before mentioned again *begun* to be opened occasionally. Respondent then told the complainant that if the door continued to be opened it would be the death of somebody, meaning those who would enter in. During the last spring or early part of summer respondent frequently heard shaking and rapping at one of the doors this occurred about once a week, generally of a Saturday night. Sometimes when this occurred complainant and respondent were awake and he would look to see who it was, and occasionally he went out and around the house but could never see any one sometimes when this would happen and when the complainant thought respondent was asleep she would gently touch him to satisfy herself that he was asleep, and upon two occasions when these *rappings* occurred and she thought respondent was asleep he knew her to get up out of bed and go out of the room and remain away from fifteen minutes to half an hour. Finally, your respondent plainly told her that there must be no more rapping at or shaking of the doors and that he could stand it no longer. She then advised respondent to sleep with his pistol and bowie-knife under his head, which, at her suggestion, he did, and the shaking and rapping at the door immediately ceased which satisfied respondent that there *head* been some other agency than the wind in shaking rapping at and opening the doors. He continued for some time to sleep with his weapons under his head and then discontinued it the rapping at and opening of the doors having likewise discontinued, and having thus slept with the weapons under his head at the suggestion and by the advice of the complainant is made a charge of complaint by her in her bill against him. Your respondent admits that he whipped the negro boy mentioned in the bill. He will here narrate all of the circumstances in relation to the whipping of the boy, and he denies every allegation in the bill to the contrary, viz:

This boy had been advanced to the complainant by her mother, and before the time alluded to, respondent had corrected him for some misconduct, upon which occasion the complainant had got into a violent passion with your respondent and abused him very much when, in order to pacify her, your respondent promised her that he would not whip the boy again, provided, she would correct him herself when he misbehaved, which she promised to do. After this, the boy was guilty of very indecent and outrageous behavior in the kitchen, for which she was required to correct him and promised to do so, but failed to comply with her promise. After this, he went into your respondent"s tobacco ground and plugged and destroyed all of his water-melons and musk-melons, and cut down not one plant but a considerably quantity of tobacco. Respondent again requested the complainant to correct him for this offense, which she promised to do, but again failed to comply with her promise. And finding that she did not intend doing so, respondent determined to whip him himself and did so, though not unmercifully as charged in the bill. This gave great offence to the complainant, and she spent nearly the whole day in abusing respondent and his relations, and when dinner came on she again set in to abusing respondent for whipping the boy, when he told her she had promised to whip the boy for his behavior in the kitchen and had not done so, and that he respondent would do so after dinner and also, whenever he again misbehaved when she replied that your respondent "should not do it to save his life, that she would send the boy to her mother"s where he would stay that she would go herself and never come back," and getting up from the table she took the boy in the direction of her mother"s and then came back without him.

19

Respondent then went in search of the boy but could not find him. And this is the whole matter about whipping the boy, the complainant had had a horse caught and saddled and was on it, and a servant had the child. Respondent asked her if she was in earnest about going, to which she returned no answer. He then took the child from the servant and asked her where the keys were, to which he got no reply. He then directed the servant to get the basket off the pommel of her saddle which had the child"s clothes in it, and as the servant approached complainant struck her with a switch and rode off. Respondent then followed her and took the basket without a word being said by either party. He then sent a boy to her for the keys not knowing they were in the basket with the child"s clothes, where they were afterwards found to be. The boy returned without any answer from her, and with only an insulting message from her mother, that your respondent "might kiss her foot."

Late in the evening, your respondent went to complainant"s mother"s to see her. When he got there her mother asked respondent to go in, which he declined, stating to her that the reasons he had received from her was sufficient reason why he should not go into her house, but told her he wished to see the complainant, and that he had only a word or two to say to her. The complainant then came out and commenced conversation, and respondent made some statement, to which she gave the lie. Respondent then told her he had not come to quarrel but to know whether she intended to return, to which she replied that she could not that evening, but that she would do so the next morning if respondent would come for her to which he replied, "that he would not that she had come off without the slightest cause, and that she must come back as she went". She then stated that she would return next morning. On her return next morning, respondent spoke to her but she would not return the salutation. He then remarked that she might as well have remained where she was, if she did not intend to speak to him. She then said she could "easily go back", and immediately commenced to abuse your respondent in the most violent manner, when to avoid her he walked off some distance to his stables, but heard her still abusing him for a considerable time. He remained away from the home for a long time and when he returned she had quieted down. In the evening he was about to start to the shop to get his mules shod, and to get a wagon to carry his wheat to market, she asked him where he was going and he told her but failing to get the wagon he did not have his mules shod and this is the whole history of his trip to her mother"s when she clandestinely sent the boy there, about which much a parade is made in her bill.

Respondent returned from his trip in endeavoring to get the wagon after sundown. After supper and after complainant had gone to bed, respondent ordered a servant to put on a kettle of water in order to wash his feet, his legs and feet being very muddy from walking through the wet during the evening. In walking about while the water was being prepared he heard that one of the servants the cook had been carrying news to her mistress about him, and about what he had promised to the little negro boy, and being determined to put a stop to such conduct on the part of his servants without saying a word to any one, he took the negro to the stable and gave her a good whipping with a pair of bridle reins. During the time the complainant came out of his house and commenced hallowing and screaming as loud as she could, and calling to your respondent to which he often answered. When he returned he found her dressed with her shawl and bonnet on. She then told respondent that she wanted to go her mother"s and was determined on it. He requested her to go to bed and remain till morning, saying to her that she could then go if she was determined on it but she refused to do so and declared that she would go that night, and ordered respondent to have a horse got for her. He then told her he had another negro to correct and that he would then have a horse got for her while he was correcting the other negro the complainant came out of the house to the front porch and screamed as loud as she could, when respondent returned she again requested him to furnish her with a horse when he again required her to stay till morning telling her that it was too damp and disagreeable to take the child out that night but if she would wait till morning she might take the child To the but she refused to do so, and going to a trunk took out a little box containing five or six dollars which she called her own. She then went to the crib where the child was and said not as if she really felt anything but in a formal and theatrical manner as if she was reciting a prepared speech, "farewell, my child, forever I never expect to see you again. May God"s blessing rest on you."

Respondent then remarked to her that if she was determined on going that he would have a horse for her immediately. But she went out of the front door without making him any reply. No such conversation as is shared in the bill about the weapons took place. Nor did respondent order his horse to be ready for him to leave at any moment and he is surprised and pained to see such a charge. He never offered complainant any violence or threatened it, nor can he believe she is at all afraid of him.

As the complainant was frequently in the habit of leaving the house under pretense of going to her mother"s and then returning, respondent thought she would soon return and paid little attention to her going out of the door at the time. But on her staying much longer than he expected, he became apprehensive that she might have gone and went in search of her, and when he reached Mr. Shelton"s he learned she was there and went in to see her. Shelton at first objected to his seeing her but upon remonstrance of your respondent and his assurance that he would not hurt a hair of her head, Shelton consented. And when your respondent did see her she poured out a tirade of her usual abuse on respondent during this interview she had expressed a determination to leave him, your respondent told her that she might take all the property that came by her and might also take the child for two years and then return it to him, when she replied to respondent that she "would not do it to save his life." Respondent then proposed that Shelton might take his horse and carry her to her mother"s, but this was not done and she remained there until her mother came and took her away.

And this your respondent avers is the whole history of complainant"s leaving him. And as it proceeded from her own fault and without any just cause on your respondent"s part he insists that she has no claim upon him. Your respondent does not believe that she abandoned him under any such apprehension as she pretends in her said bill, but he believes it was in execution of a *preconcerted* plan between her mother and herself, for her to abandon him under such apparent circumstances as would be calculated to cover all her guilt from the public eye. He is induced to this belief because he is well assured they had for some time kept up a secret correspondence, for he, by accident saw one of complainant"s notes to her mother written at a time when respondent"s sister from Georgia was on a visit to him, in which she complained of bad treatment on that day and expressed a doubt whether she could live with him although not one angry word had passed between them. The only offence charged to respondent was that he had given some preserves to one of his sister"s children about which she said in her note that respondent, "was making himself an ass over his sister and her children" and such was complainant"s conduct that

21

respondent was forced to request his sister in order to secure her from being hurt and mortified not to repeat her visit.

As to the matter charged in the bill in relation to complainant and the said Gilbert, your respondent will make a simple statement of facts, *vis* :

Shortly after her marriage respondent discovered that complainant was very fond of being in Gilbert"s company and visited his mother where he lived, when she refused to visit elsewhere though desired to do so by respondent and when in his company she was very familiar with Gilbert and took a great many liberties with him. Your respondent thought nothing of this at first and attributed it merely to her gay and lively disposition. Gilbert was a "frequent visitor at respondent"s house, and he and complainant were in the habit of playing cards in which respondent sometimes joined this familiarity continuing and seeming to get more close. Your respondent thought she showed too much liberty of conduct and might subject herself to injurious remarks though he himself still thought no evil and as hereinbefore stated requested her to change her deportment to him and decline receiving his attentions and visits. After this your respondent discovered that she was in the habit of receiving his visits in your respondent"s absence. And was in the habit of taking the cards from the pack marking them and sending them in a particular direction by the little negro boy and after his return strolling off in the same direction by herself and remaining absent for a considerable time and one time on a Sabbath morning nearly the whole day, and when your respondent would ask her where she had been she would get into a passion and tell him "it was none of his business". On one occasion your respondent himself saw her take a card and mark it and go into another room and give it to the negro boy and send him off with it. Your respondent, thereupon determined to see if he could see where the boy went with the cards and what he did with them, went in the same direction the boy usually went and concealed himself to see what would come of it. Sometimes afterwards she started in the same direction but in going she called or beckoned a negro woman to her, and learning, as he supposed, that your respondent had gone that way, she stopped and concealed herself in the *lapse* of a tree that had been blown down and remained there about an hour and as your respondent did not return or show himself she returned to the house. And from circumstances and an investigation your respondent satisfied himself that the cards were sent and deposited in a particular hollow tree from whence they were taken by the said Gilbert. And while this was going on the rapping at the doors took place at night as hereinafter mentioned. Your respondent submits that under these circumstances he had just grounds for suspecting the complainant of improper intercourse with the said Gilbert. And he believes that she was either guilty or acted in the way she did for the purpose of inducing the belief on the mind of respondent that she was, in order to induce him to do or say something that might give her a pretest for carrying out her scheme of leaving him and throwing the odium of their separation on him.

Your respondent says it is not true that he possesses the amount of property set forth in the bill. The land therein mentioned does not belong to him, but to his father, and he is in possession of it and remains upon it merely by his father"s permission. Nor is it true that the complainant had the advancements pretended by her bill. Besides the small boy who was valued when advanced at the price of $350.00, she had only a bed, a bureau, a cow and a colt and six hundred dollars advanced in money. Respondent does not believe that anything more of it was brought into his possession by the complainant than the negro boy and the bed. But whatever she brought respondent is willing for her to take away.

But your respondent is unwilling for to have the custody, naming and education of his infant child, because she is wholly unfit to have the control, education and moral training of a female but he was willing and offered to let her keep the child until it attained a sufficient age to be removed but this, as before stated, she indignantly refused. The parade made in the bill about the tender age of the child and of its being "dependent on its mother"s breast for support" is all pretense. Because the child has been raised thus far principally by hand and not from its mother"s breast, and she had been in the habit of frequently of going from home and leaving it to be attended to by others, and fed from the bottle when it was more of then it is now and stood more in need of a mother"s care.

Your respondent feels greatly aggrieved by the harsh proceedings that have been had against him by the complainant and her friends in this case, in having taken his child and sequestered all of his estate without any just grounds and without affording any opportunity to contest it or show cause against it. Your respondent is advised that the bill of the plaintiff does not show any ground for a divorce, and that injunction awarded in the cause and the order made for the benefit of the complainant on her ex parte statement were improvidently made and ought to be discharged.

He is advised that although the statute provides that the court or judge in vacation, pending a suit for divorce may make any order that may be proper for the support of the woman and maintenance of the suit, and for securing the estate of the man, yet he is advised that such is not proper and ought not to be made without the bill shows a cause for divorce, and without some proof of the facts for which the divorce is asked, so as to show to the court that there were some reasonable grounds for the suit. And that the statements of the bill verified by the affidavit of the plaintiff does not afford sufficient evidence for that purpose as the act expressly provides that neither the statements of the bill or answer are to be rewarded in deciding the cause.

But even if the statements of the bill making a proper case verified by such affidavit was sufficient for the purpose, your respondent submits that the bill of a difficult affidavit in this case if it had been made a proper case for the jurisdiction of the court are not sufficient for the foundation of such an order. The facts in the bill if true are within the knowledge of the complainant and are set forth to be within her knowledge yet she does not make affidavit to their truth but merely to her belief and the affidavits of the other two persons are made altogether upon faith. They merely state that they believe the facts of the bill to be true without stating they have any knowledge of them or the ground upon which their belief is founded. Your respondent is advised that the testimony of any member of witnesses, however respectable, that they "verily believe the facts stated in the bill to be true", would not upon the hearing he rewarded for a moment, and that no court would upon such testimony decree one cent in favor of the complainant. And he is advised that it ought not to have any greater effect when offered ex parte.

Your respondent therefor, prays that the said injunction and order made in vacation be discharged. And having answered, he prays to be hence dismissed, etc.

Franklin County, to-wit:

This day the above named James R. Clement made oath before me, that the facts in the foregoing answer, so far as they are stated to be upon his knowledge are true, and so far as they are stated upon his belief or information he believes them to be true.

Given under my hand, this the 20th day of October, 1859
      JAS. PATTERSON
      Chancery Commissioner of the Circuit Court of Franklin County. A
copy-Teste, H.E. Carper, Clerk

"THAT SCRAPE AT SANDY LEVEL"
September 13, 1859

A shooting incident occurred at Sandy Level, Pittsylvania County only two weeks after Victoria C. Clement filed her Complaint for Divorce and prior to James R. Clement"s Answer. There were no documents found regarding this incident, the only records are found in the depositions and James R. Clement"s Will

"On a former occasion at the taking of some depositions on behalf of the plaintiff at Sandy Level in Pittsylvania *county*, while the defendant was sitting quietly engaged in a conversation with a gentleman he was fired upon by Wm. P. Gilbert a person implicated in his domestic difficulties and severely wounded while in a sitting posture. This attack was made at a time and under circumstances when he Jas. R. Clement was not expecting it and I feel justified in believing that one or more of the persons engaged in the affair at Dickinson"s store, on the 25th of last February, aided and abetted Gilbert in the attack made on that occasion."
    James R. Clement

"The foregoing Deposition of Wm. P. Gilbert, was *This* day subscribed as far as gone but was not concluded in consequence of medical advice. That it was imprudent to put the witness under examination the said witness being wounded by a pistol shot. {can"t read}. The farther taking of said deposition was postponed by mutual consent of the parties.
    C.L.   Powell   J.P.
    Richard Parker J.P.

"I James R. Clement of the County of Franklin and State of Virginia contemplating the end of life from assassination or attack from my enemies such as I experienced at Sandy Level in the *county* of Pittsylvania on the 14th *Inst* but being of sound and disposing mind and memory do make this my last will and testament hereby revoking all others"
    James R. Clement's Will {filed less than two weeks after he was shot at Sandy Level}

"You have stated that Dr. Clement, the father of James R. Clement said when you asked for the horse that he wished you would go {to Sandy Level}. Now state why he said he wanted you to go

The old *Doct* said if Ralph should happen to get shot or anything of that sort if I would take care of him or let him know

State if you were at James R. Clements on the day James & Johnston Clement were said to have been shot at Sandy Level and if you were if said Dr Clement asked you to go there any time during the day and if he did say what for

Yes I was there on the day they was said to have been shot at work and David Williams came and told me that James Clement said he wanted me to fetch him his buggy to fetch him home. Then I started down there some and the old *Doct* and William and met them fetching them home in a wagon when we met them the old Doctor got me and William to go on to see what had become of Ralph and we met him coming and we turned back."
Shirwood Y. Shelton {Johnston Clement"s Overseer}

VICTORIA C. CLEMENT AND SAMUEL B. BERGER

"State whether or not the said Victoria C. Clement was not but a few weeks before marriage with James R. Clement, from an understanding in your family, engaged to your Brother Samuel B. Berger and whether or not you ever heard a report that the said Victoria C. was not attached to the said James R"

Overruled by the Court
George T. Berger

{Note: Victoria C. Clement later married Samuel Southard Berger, the marriage record could not be found. A picture of her tombstone can be found on the Internet at findagrave.com}

THREATS AND RUMORS

"I had a conversation with James Clement on Friday {February 24}before the occurrence took place on Saturday. I was standing in the door. He came out by me and *sorter* touched me on the arm and I followed him out and he asked me if I thought that the *Witcher's* would break him up yet. I told him that I didn"t know whether they would or not but if I had heard the truth that I thought that they ought to break his neck. And he asked me then if I had heard both tales and I told him nothing more than *rumurs* in the neighborhood and he said he thought so too if they be true reports or if the reports were true. I remarked then that I was going home. He told me not to leave that the fun hadn"t commenced yet. I told him that such fun as they generally had didn"t suit me and he told me that I wouldn"t be hurt - not to be afraid. I stepped back to the door and nodded my head to Mr. James Rice. He came out and I told him to lets go home and he said that we would go home. He started home and Mr. {James} Clement was walking backwards and forwards in the porch-floor and he remarked again not to leave that the fun hadn"t commenced yet. I remarked to him again that that was a kind of fun that I didn"t want to see, and I told him that from what I heard that they were bad marksmen that they generally shot too low. He Mr. {James} Clement remarked that from what they told him that he took pretty good aim at his man over yonder that he struck him somewhere about here putting his hand somewhere near about the groin and the ball struck a money purse or *port-monie*, I don"t recollect which, and ranged around towards his hip. Mr. Shack Law was standing there at the time and then him and Mr.

{James} Clement went off together and went into what I call a private conversation as there was no person about there and me and Mr. Rice went off home"
Silas W. Evans

"Wash Evans, George Sampson, James Rice and myself were together on Friday evening at the end of the porch at Dickinson"s, and in a conversation, James Clement came out and spoke to me and joined us in the conversation. Wash Evans I think remarked that he was going home or wanted to go home. James says, „oh no hold on and see the fun" which caused me to take notice of him James Clement. Which from that conversation led to the conversation between Wash Evans and I couldn"t say whether James Rice joined in it, though he was present and heard it in relation to shooting and as to the precise words I am not sure that I could give the precise words but I think that Wash Evans remarked to him that he „didn"t wish to join in such fun as this" for he generally shot too low. By some remarks I made to James Clement I drew him off from the crowd. He walked to me and threw his arm around my shoulder. We started off down the lane together in the direction of Mr. Finney"s

You speak of a conversation with Robert N. Powell, in which you told him that you heard James Clement make a remark that induced you to fear a *reencounter*. What was the remark

I said to him „Jim why do you make such remark as this" Says he „they are preparing for something Says I Jim as I have always told you before you are too excitable and you are excited now" He said „Jack they are going to kill me" Says I „Jim what in the world do you mean by making such remarks as that" Says he „I saw Mr. Dabney give Sile Dudley two pistols" Says I „Jim *its* all humbuggery and you be cool and deliberate and have no fighting" Says he „Jack you have always given me good advice and I will take it and so as I have always done and I will not be the aggressor but the defender and if I am shot at I"ll be damned if I don"t shoot the man that shoots at me" Says I „Jim, if all of them will act the way that you have promised to act there will be no fighting. Right there we parted"
John C. Law

"State if ever you had any conversation with S.Y. Shelton concerning the deposition he gave at this place, in the suit of John A. Smith, next friend of Victoria A. Clement, against James R. Clement, and if you did, state that conversation and all about it

I heard Mr. Shelton speaking of his deposition. He stated to me that he did not give a right deposition. He said the Mr. Witchers taken him out and told him they had stated things, and some had been stated from his house, and he had to give the same testimony or bad might be the consequences. He said he did not do Mr. Clement justice on that occasion he was *affraid* of the Mr. *Witchers* he said that he did not know how soon they put a ball in him or kill him

State if he said anything about certain looks and frowns he received while giving in his testimony. If he did, what did he say of them

He said they looked at him very cross at times and *helt thir* hands on *thir* revolvers"
George Samson

"Having stated that you did not know any cause for Capt. Witcher firing at Mr. Clement state whether or not you did not know of an angry family *law suit* and *feiud* between the parties and their immediate relations

I had understood there was such a suit as that going on and supposed that they were taking that deposition for that purpose as for knowing the fact I did not"
John C. Hutcherson

"Was not the law suit of which you have spoken a subject of deep feeling among the parties to it and their immediate connections and of an implacable feud between Vincent Witcher and his near relations and the deceased and their near relations

So far as I am informed it was a subject of deep feeling among all"
Colonel Madison Carter

"I had a conversation Saturday, in the early part of the day, with James Clement. I was out there in the end of the porch at the store. I spoke to James Clement. „The taking of the depositions was a slow business.‟ He said, „yes‟. I spoke of going home and he said it wasn‟t *worth while* to be in a hurry that they would settle the hash after a while probably. That is all the conversation I had with him

State whether or not, at any previous time, you had any conversation with any of the said Clements about any difficulty they expected to have with the said defendants, or either of them

I have talked with James Clement several times since that scrape they had at Sandy Level. I don‟t know that he said that he expected to have any difficulty. I recollect having a conversation with him at Muse‟s he was saying to me there that I had understood he *reconed* how bad they had treated him that old Vincent Witcher was the evil of it and he wished he might die before it was settled that it might save him the trouble of killing him

In your reply to the question before the last, did you not mean to state that you never heard James Clement say that he would kill any of them if they would let him alone

I did. He never said that he would kill any of them

Did you hear James Clement say that he would kill Capt. Witcher or any of his party unless they would let him alone

No. I never heard him say that he would kill any of them"
JAMES M. GIBSON

"During your stay did you not see any abrupt conduct respecting the depositions between James and Ralph Clement?

Yes I saw them fall out and saw Mr Ralph Clement get up and say to James Clement if he didn‟t hush his mouth go and sit down and let him alone that he would quit and go home.

Has Capt Witcher the reputation of being a brave and spirited man?

I think he has

Is it likely from Capt Witchers character or spirit that he would allow any man wantonly to insult him without resenting it?

I don't think he would
Have you not heretofore had a difficulty with Mr Ralph A Clement

Yes we had a difficulty. Mr Clement forced that difficulty on me whether I would or not. I tried to beg out I got up and left twice during the investigation of this matter and finally disputed my word the third time. I had stood it just as long as I could stand it and remarked to him that he had disputed my word the third time and he shouldn't do it any more. He gathered a chair {and} struck at me. I caught the chair jerked it away from him gathered him by the head. He never whipped me. We afterwards made friends and my *feeling* were perfectly good towards him to the day of his death"

"State if you ever had any conversation with James Clement during the taking of the depositions in relation to any difficulty with Vincent Witcher or any of his family which he expected to have during the taking of the depositions

I had some with him Friday morning and he said he expected the Witchers would fight Thursday but they appeared to be cool as cucumbers I think that is about all he said"
    A.L.H. Muse

"State if you ever had any conversation with James Clement during the taking of the depositions in relation to any difficulty with Vincent Witcher or any of his family which he expected to have during the taking of the depositions

I had some with him Friday morning and he said he expected the Witchers would fight Thursday but they appeared to be cool as cucumbers I think that is about all he said

Were you present when James Clement started off to attend to taking depositions from home

Yes I was

State whether he armed himself

Yes he did"
    James F. Powell

"THE DAMNED LIE"

"On Thursday last, James Clement came to my house and requested me to come to Dickinson"s to take depositions as a justice. I came and commenced taking the deposition of Mrs. Shelton. I did not get through with her deposition adjourned over until next day, 10 o"clock, when her deposition was completed. After closing Mrs. Shelton"s deposition on Saturday about one o"clock, Vincent Witcher asked to have the taking of depositions postponed until Monday, as he did not believe that there would be any chance to get through with them that day that he wished to go home that he lived some fifteen miles. Ralph Clement objected to it said he had a female witness there and insisted on going on and taking her deposition. I decided to go on. There was a conversation commenced between Capt. Witcher and Ralph Clement about that time, which I did not consider there was any malice about more than common. I *ris* up out my chair summoning in my mind, the oath to administer to the witness. I heard the report of a pistol or gun, and from that it continued mighty fast. In a minute or so, there was a heap of fog or smoke, looking towards the door that leads out of that room into the store, I saw Mr. Samuel Swanson striking with a stick left that room and went into the store. I then went out and commanded the crowd to take charge of *them* men. In making my statement in regard to taking the depositions, alluded to, I erred in saying that I commenced taking Mrs. Shelton"s deposition. I commenced with George Sampson and the first day and part of the next was consumed in taking his deposition

I went out in the porch and summoned the crowd to come and take charge of *them* men. In this time, Capt. Witcher or Vincent Witcher come to the door and remarked that I need not be afraid, that there *wan't* a man in there that was *a guine* to run that they *want* running stock. I never heard any man say that he had taken part in the fight. The above is all I heard Capt. Witcher say on the subject. He came to the door that leads from the counting room into the porch, as well as I recollect"

Robert Mitchell, Justice

"That I was not in the room when the first pistol was fired. I had been in there a moment or two previous. When they were about to proceed to take the deposition of Miss Bennett. Capt. Vincent Witcher renewed his motion for an adjournment of taking the deposition of Miss Bennett addressing himself to the court remarked substantially as well as I recollect. If justice could be obtained or was likely to be obtained by commencing the taking of that deposition when it could not be completed on that evening and leaving the witness in the care and control of the opposite party to be conversed with as well as I recollect until the next week or Monday. To which Mr. Ralph A. Clement replied that the witness was not under his care or *controul*, and remarked that the court might take charge of the witness himself put her at any other place or send her to jail if the law would allow him. Capt. Witcher then said, as well as I recollect, that he had understood or been informed that Ralph A. Clement had brought her, the witness, there that day under his care and *controul* to which Ralph A. Clement replied, "if any person says I brought her here under my care or *controul* it is a lie.". I then shook my head at Ralph A. Clement, turned and started out of the room. Before I got out of the room I heard Capt. Witcher say, "make your supposition or charge", as well as I recollect, "more definite or explicit if you like." About the time I got to the door leading from the counting-room into the store, or perhaps one step inside of the store-room, a rush of persons came against me and threw me off to the left of the entrance way at that time the firing commenced in the room. As soon as I heard the firing

29

commence I wheeled about and endeavored to make my entrance back into the room, but as often as I attempted it I was thrown back by persons rushing out, until the firing had nearly ceased. When I entered the room I saw James R. Clement lying dead on the floor, and some gentleman"s arm with a pistol in his hand, not more than two feet and-a-half, I think, from the body of James R. Clement, fire the pistol at him. I saw not the slightest movement in the body. I then passed over him, and a little farther in the room I saw William C. Clement *lieing* dead. I heard Ralph A. Clement complaining at the farther side of the room partly under the writing desk and partly not. I went to him, took him up and set him on the floor, and asked two or three gentlemen to assist me in laying him on the bed they did so. I remained with him, except a few moments, until he died. While I was endeavoring to enter the door from the store-room while the firing was going on, there was a vacancy occasioned by persons passing out that I saw into the room, at which moment I saw James R. Clement standing on the bed near the *centre* thereof, about three feet and towards us in a slightly curved position forward. I saw him no more the aperture closed until I saw him *lieing* dead at the foot of the bed

At that time, I did not, except so far as Ralph A. Clement was concerned. I endeavored, as well as I could, ascertain the number and locality of his wounds, to see whether they were mortal or not. I found on him six if not seven wounds two of which, were in his right shoulder a little back of the front part of his arm one across the left side of his head above the ear one on the right side of the spine, passing, as I judged, through the right kidney one through his left *fore* finger, and a glance on the left arm between the shoulder and elbow, as well as I recollect. After the death of Ralph A. Clement, I examined the body of William Clement very partially. I saw a hole shot in the bone of his right eye, which I considered mortal. I did not strip him at that time. After the body was stripped by the coroner, I saw upon his body various mortal wounds the number I do not know., not having counted them. He had a stab with a bowie-knife or dirk in his whiskers, striking about where the teeth entered the jaw-bone on the right jaw immediately under the jaw- bone there was a long and apparently deep gash on his right side below the ribs there was a gash through which a portion of his bowels had *protuded*. He had two other stabs that I recollect one on his right breast another just under the collar-bone, apparently inflicted with an elevated hand some three or four bullet-holes, or perhaps more. I did not count them around and about the *centre* of his chest. He had also a considerable cut on the muscle of the left arm. As to James R. Clement, I did not examine his wounds with as much particularity as I did the others, from the fact that he had some wounds in the breast that I believed had penetrated his heart, from the profusion of blood that had escaped. I saw upon his head near the top rather on the right side, where he had received two blows apparently from a stick. I saw across the right side of his forehead above the eye another bruise. I saw on his left arm several bruises that I judged were caused by a stick

Colonel Madison Carter

"There was a moment"s pause and both men *ris* and clapped their hands to their bosoms, as if they intended to draw their weapons. While they were in the act of drawing weapons I heard the report of a pistol, that drew my attention from them. I looked towards where the sound was and saw James Clement upon the bed rather in a crooked condition, as if he was rising, with his pistol presented and the smoke boiling up before his face. My attention was then drawn from him by a scuffle with Ralph A. Clement and Addison Witcher, and pretty quick I saw Samuel Swanson and James Clement engaged - Swanson striking with his stick and Clement firing at him. I looked at them until I heard three fires from James Clement"s pistol. My attention was again drawn to Ralph A. Clement and Addison Witcher saying to *some one* "don"t shoot me - shoot the damned rascal. I then heard the report of a pistol right close by and saw the man that fired ii, I took to be Oliver Smith. I am satisfied that it was him. The next thing I saw was Capt. Witcher with his pistol presented towards James Clement and fired. James Clement fell. I then turned my eye back where Ralph Clement was, and he was sinking down rather on his elbow. I heard him say that he was „a dead man - they have killed me for nothing". After leaving the room, I jo saw John A. Smith with his bowie-knife in his hand with it stained with blood"

Benjamin F. Cooper

"Captain Witcher was sitting on the other side of the fire-place immediately after Ralph Clement said them Captain Witcher rose from his chair and commenced putting his hand in his bosom and drew his pistol out and stepped a step or two towards him Ralph Clement and fired it right over my head directly that was fired there was several others but I know not who they were. Ralph Clement sprang from his chair where he was sitting taking hold of each side of his coat he looked like he was aiming to open his coat and I darted under the writing desk that was near me and saw that some gentleman had hold of Ralph Clement but do not know who it was as to his face I did not use it. He says, „shoot him again God damn him kill him". He made several remarks „I am a dead man" Ralph Clement made the remark that he was a dead man. The fire by Captain Witcher was the first fire made in the room."

Elizabeth Bennett

"When Ralph Clement got up, where was Capt. Witcher, and what did he do and say

He was sitting in a chair on the opposite side of the fire-place from where he, Ralph Clement, was sitting. As Ralph Clement sat down Capt. Witcher arose up out of his chair and put his hand in his bosom and stepped a step or two, advancing towards him, and drew his pistol out and fired it over my head"

Edney Shelton

"I made my way to the door as fast as I could. Just before I got to the door I heard a pistol fire in my rear, I did not know who fired it. Before I cleared the door there was two or three other pistols fired in quick succession, and then the firing was very rapid at first towards the end of the combat were not so frequent, and shortly the firing instantly ceased. After the firing had ceased I saw Capt. Witcher and Addison Witcher and Samuel Swanson, John A. Smith and Oliver Smith all coming out of the counting-room into the porch. John A. Smith had a bowie-knife in hand. He paused *near by* me, his coat on fire on his right shoulder. I brushed out the fire with my own hand. There was three bullet-holes in his coat. I examined them and I discovered that two of the holes *was* made with the same bullet but it did not touch the flesh. I think the other bullet went into the shoulder, passed through to the front side of the arm and lodged near the surface. I saw it taken out. Oliver Smith passed on by me also. He appeared to be holding his arm. He left there and came on towards Brook"s with the rest of the company. After they had left I returned to the counting-room where the combat had taken place. On entering the counting-room by the door leading from the store-room to the counting-room, I saw James R. Clement lying dead. His head near the door leading into the store out of the counting-room his feet extended towards the bed he lying on his back a little inclined to the right his face turned to the right so that the side of his

31

face same near the floor there was a considerable pool of blood by his side and from his appearance seemed to be *severly* wounded in the breast he was lying with his right hand across his breast, with the hilt of a bowie-knife grasped in his hand – the bowie-knife was in the scabbard. I think there was a five-shooter lying near his side. After viewing him, I saw William Clement lying on the floor some little distance from him, perhaps about the middle of the room. He was also dead. One eye appeared to be shot out, the ball entering the outside corner of his eye. I didn't at that time discover any other wound, but this breast was a little bloody the eye that was shot was smartly stained with powder, or powder-burnt. I then turned my eyes to Ralph Clement. He was complaining very much and down upon the floor. I can't say whether he was lying or rather crumpled up, getting with his hands on the floor. Colo. Carter and some other gentlemen were in the room at the time. We took him off of the floor and laid him upon the bed. I discovered when we laid him on the bed that there was two bullet holes in the back of his right shoulder, I think his head was bleeding. I think, from the cut of a glancing ball - which side I cannot now say. After lying upon the bed a while complaining greatly of his back, Carter pulled up his *cloths*. I saw a bullet-hole in the right side of the spine. From the appearance of the bullet- hole and its apparent direction I thought it likely that it had fractured the right kidney. I think he
lingered something like two hours and died"
Charles Powell

"I heard Vincent Witcher suggesting the propriety of adjourning over until Monday, on the grounds that the examination of the witness could not be got through with that afternoon, and that she would consequently be in the hands of the opposite party. At that point, I think that Ralph Clement remarked that she could be placed under the care of the court or in jail, he *did'nt* care which. The court, Robert Mitchell, remarked that he should do nothing of the kind. Vincent Witcher still pressed his desire that it should be continued, on the grounds that the witness would not be under the care of the opposite party that the opposite {party} might not have the advantage of dictating to {the witness} as they might have if the examination was commenced and adjourned over unfinished. Ralph Clement remarked, that she was not under his keeping or under his care. Vincent Witcher replied that whoever said that told a damned lie. Ralph Clement rose to his feet when he made that remark, but immediately resumed his seat. Vincent Witcher said you had better make your remark more direct. Ralph Clement made some remark that I could not catch, but immediately there was a general stir in the room, and a firing of pistols. I did not see any one shoot. I do not know who fired first. I do not know who fired at all. My first effort was to get out of the room. I heard as many as four shots before I succeeded. That is all I can say that I saw or heard at that time. I remained out at the end of the house until the firing had ceased. Persons were coming out. Among others my attention was attracted to a young man particularly, who seemed to be in pain, holding one arm, with a knife or dirk in the other hand, it bloody. John Anthony Smith, was the man alluded to *some one* accompanied him to the house so far as I saw I could not say that I recognized *any one* else, particular under the excitement.

I found James Clement lying dead near the door in a considerable pool of blood with his knife grasped in his hand unsheathed a little further in the room near the center I saw William Clement lying dead he lay in somewhat a coiled position, with his arm crooked but rather extended, the fore-finger pointing straight with a pistol lying across his arm, about half way between the wrist and the elbow I made no examination of the pistol nor did I take it in my hand a little further still in the room I saw Ralph Clement lying on the floor, his head supported by a man by the name of Baker I believe apparently badly wounded Colo. Carter seemed to be affording him what relief he could by bathing his face, I believe, with camphor, or spirits and camphor. Colo. Carter Mr. Baker and myself and Charles Powell I believe assisted to put him on the bed he appeared to suffer very much - something like an hour and a half from that time he died"

Jacob Mackenhamer

"I suppose that I got into the counting-room of Dickinson"s store on Saturday last about one o"clock. When I stepped into the door I saw Ralph Clement sitting by the side of a little table seemed to be in the act of writing or looking over papers I went around and took a stand near the fire-place with my back to the fire. The first thing I knew of Capt. Witcher he was sitting at my right side against the bed and said something about the deposition of a certain lady sitting before the fire. I thought Capt. Witcher was disposed to have the deposition taking adjourned over until Monday. Mr. Ralph A. Clement seemed desirous it should go on. Capt. Witcher was making some remarks to the justice his remarks was I think he was opposed to going into it without there was time to complete it and he didn"t think there was and I think said something about the witness would be in the hands of the opposite party. Clement remarked that she could be placed under guard or anywhere satisfactory that he shouldn"t be with her. Capt. Witcher"s reply was that she had been under their control for some time. Clement said that any man said she had been under his control was a liar. Capt. Witcher paused, I thought, a very short time asked him to make that more direct or personal or if he did make that direct, or personal, or something to that effect. Capt. Witcher then commenced rising up in a position which caused me to believe that he was fixing to get arms, raising his hands. I then aimed to walk out and look back and see what they done before I stopped to look back a pistol was fired. I pursued on and immediately another pistol was fired. I was passing on and as I got near the door I rather turned my head and saw the flash of a pistol - the ball passed through a lock of my hair and then I left. After the shooting was over I went into the house by the end door of the porch I stepped over James Clement lying before the door dead. William Clement was lying near the middle of the floor dead. Ralph A. Clement lying near, or rather against the writing desk he seemed to be very much wounded and said he was bound to die"

John C. Hutcherson

"I was in the counting-room at the time the affray occurred consequently I know nothing of the circumstances under which James Clement came to his death. I was out of doors some twenty or twenty-five steps from the scene of action when the firing commenced as soon as I heard the firing I started to the room got near the end of the porch met a number of gentlemen rushing out of the room about that time the firing was going on furiously. I advanced no farther toward the room until the firing ceased - I then went into the room. The first thing that attracted my attention was James R. Clement lying on the floor with his head near the door leading from the store into the counting-room and appeared to be entirely dead. I could not well pass into the room without stepping over his head and shoulders. After looking at him a few seconds I stepped over him and William Clement was lying on the floor and appeared also to be dead. At about that time Ralph A. Clement was also on the floor near the writing desk and seemed to be struggling to get up which he did not succeed in doing and declared himself a murdered man or a dying man I am not certain which at that time but am certain he afterwards said several times that he was a dying man. A few minutes after Colo. Carter and some other gentlemen took him up

33

and put him on the bed where he lived perhaps two hours or two-and-half and died. I saw him die

Soon after he {Ralph Clement} was laid on the bed he seemed to become a little more composed he then called for the magistrate and said he wished to make a dying declaration - the magistrate was not in the room at that time, that I now recollect. Some minutes afterwards he said he wanted to see Robert Mitchell. Mr. Mitchell then went to his bed-side, and he went on to make a tolerable lengthy statement to Mr. Mitchell, the magistrate, and said it was his dying declaration Mr. Mitchell turned *roun* the bed and came to where I was, and I suggested to the magistrate that it would be best to reduce that declaration to writing that I thought it was his privilege to make such a declaration, and the law required it to be in writing thereupon Mr. Mitchell requested me to do the writing. I refused to do so told him I never had done such a thing. He then turned to Mr. Mackenheimer, asked Mr. Mackenheimer to do it Mr. Mackenheimer also refused to do it. They came to me a second time to do it and I done it. The following is a copy of the paper referred to:

"The following is the declaration of Ralph A. Clement, as his dying declaration, relative to the shooting of himself and brothers, made before me, Robert Mitchell a justice of the peace for Franklin *county*, this 25th day of February, 1860, that is:
     'I never attempted to draw an arm. Addison Witcher *catched* me and held me around the waist and arms and told them to come and shoot me – a damned rascal. I was shot several times while in that fix, and he held me until I fell – numbers of pistols were fired at me then'."
     Gresham Choice

WOUNDS

Re: William Clement"s wounds, "It was immediately over and across the carotid artery whether it reached to it or went through it I cannot say. I opened the wound and saw it was very deep, but did not farther examine it"
     Colonel Madison Carter

"At that time I discovered but one wound, and that was near the right eye {William Clement"s}. I was a witness in the room before the coroner"s inquest after the body was stripped. I then saw a number of wounds on his body. He had one wound on the neck just under the jaw a lengthy rash it appeared to be inflicted by a bowie-knife. He was stabbed in several places, at one of which, his intestines had come out. I think on the right side just below his ribs. I can"t undertake to describe the gun shot or bullet wounds, but there was a number of them"
     Gresham Choice

"I assisted in taking off the belt. I found his {Ralph Clement"s} pistol in the pocket of his belt, and while drawing the belt from under the body assisted by Colo. Carter he took the pistol out of its pocket. I did not take hold of the pistol nor do I know whether it was loaded or not. I saw no knife in the belt

I saw him {Ralph} between the time of his being wounded and his death and he appeared to retain his senses I should say up to within some fifteen minutes of the time of his dying and think he retained his senses as long as he did his speech
Gresham Choice

"Oliver Smith was wounded near the left *rist* by a pistol-ball on the back part of the arm. Samuel Swanson had a slight wound on one of his arms, I don''t recollect which, apparently __ {sic} with a ball

You speak of bullet-holes in the clothes of John A. Smith and Samuel Swanson. How many bullet-holes and cuts were there upon the dead bodies of the deceased

I couldn''t say how many. I saw but one cut. I didn''t examine the bodies. The cut was in the side

of William Clement just below the ribs – a pretty severe cut, the intestines protruded out a little"
Charles Powell

WEAPONS

"Ralph A. Clement had a five shooter and a small hand dirk William C. Clement had a five shooter and a bowie-knife James R. Clement had the same they had no other arms except their pocket-knives that I know of on that and each previous day
Colonel Madison Carter

"I examined their weapons. I found the pistol of James R. Clement entirely discharged - every barrel – it was a five-shooter. His bowie-knife had not been drawn from the scabbard. William C. Clement''s pistol, a five-shooter, also, two barrels had been discharged his bowie-knife had not been drawn from the scabbard. Ralph A. Clement''s pistol, a five-shooter, also had not been taken from his belt nor fired his dirk, a small hand dirk, had not been taken from his pocket, nor had the newspaper scabbard, tied with a string, been removed"
Colonel Madison Carter

"He, also, saw John Anthony Smith come out of the counting-room with a pistol in one hand and a bowie-knife in the other, soon after the firing ceased and that the knife and hand of said Smith was bloody"
John B. Law

{This is the cover of the book published June 14, 1860 by Dr. George W. Clement.
That book did not include all the testimony or all the information from all the Court documents.}

THE EVIDENCE in the case of The Commonwealth

Versus

VINCENT WITCHER, ADDISON WITCHER, SAMUEL SWANSON,
JOHN A. SMITH AND VINCENT O. SMITH

{Page damaged} and murder of
RALPH A., WM. C. and JAMES R. CLEMENT
On the 25th of February 1860

AS TAKEN BEFORE BENJ. F. COOPER, ESQ.
AT DICKENSON'S STORE, FRANKLIN COUNTY, VIRGINIA

Lynchburg, Virginia
Printed at the Virginia Job Office
1860

"TO THE PUBLIC"
Dr. George W. Clement, Sr.

As many statements, ex parte and false, wholly and in part, in relation to the unfortunate difficulty between my son, the late James R. Clement, and his wife which ended so tragically in the death of him and two of my other sons Ralph A. and Wm. C. Clement, on the 25th of February last, have been given to the world, through the newspapers – I feel it due to their memory, and as an act of justice to their surviving friends, to present, in this form, a full and impartial statement of the whole matter, so far as the materials in my power will enable me to do.

After the deliberation, I have concluded to present certified copies of the bill Victoria C. Clement, by John A. Smith, her next friend in the Circuit Court of the *county* of Franklin and the answer of James R. Clement thereto and all the depositions taken by her to prove the allegations of said bill and the depositions taken by him so far as they went. The depositions of one of the most material witnesses was abruptly broken off by the *tragical* death of James R. Clement and the friends of the deceased cannot now avail themselves of the benefit of the testimony of that witness, which they confidently believe would have sustained substantially almost every important allegation in his answer, so far as her means of information extended. In addition to this witness there was another which the defendant intended to examine who had also been living in his family a portion of the time during the unfortunate and unhappy marriage, by whom he had every reason to believe he could have proven similar facts. And there were various other persons, who not having as ample means of information as the two witnesses referred to, would still have proven similar facts that would have materially corroborated their testimony, and sustained other allegations of his answer. And there were various other persons, who not having as ample means of information as the two witnesses referred to, would still have proven isolated facts that would have materially corroborated their testimony, and sustained other allegations of his answer.

From circumstances which had transpired previously to the taking of the depositions on that occasion, and from what took place on the 25th of February. I am forced reluctantly as it may be to the conclusion that the horrid and woful sic tragedy enacted on that day was the result of a pre-conceived determination on the part of the plaintiff's friends, not to prevent the witness, Elizabeth Bennett, to testify in the case, if they could prevent it. That much was the fact, I think will be apparent to every unprejudiced mind that will carefully examine the testimony and all the circumstances connected with this unfortunate and lamentable affair.

On a former occasion at the taking of some depositions on behalf of the plaintiff at Sandy Level, in Pittsylvania *county*, while the defendant was sitting quietly engaged in a conversation with a gentleman, he was fired upon by Wm. P. Gilbert, a person implicated in his domestic difficulties, and severely wounded while in a sitting posture. This attack was made at a time and under circumstances when he, Jas. R. Clement was not expecting it and I feel justified in believing that one or more of the persons engaged in the affair at Dickinson's store, on the 25th of last February, aided and abetted Gilbert in the attack made on that occasion.

It is a matter of deep regret, that the evidence was not taken down on the trial of the prisoners before the Examining Court, and that I have to rely entirely upon the depositions taken before the

Examining Court, and that I have to rely entirely upon the depositions taken before the Committing Magistrate. It is, however, substantially the same in every material particular, and no new witnesses were called except a few testified to some unimportant points. I regret it, because it may be said that this is not a transcript of the testimony which was before the court that discharged the prisoners. But that it gives all the facts as elicited on the examination I honestly and firmly believe, I have thought it best to publish the evidence precisely as taken by the Justice - not to vary or change even the phrase except to punctuate it, in order that it may be intelligible.

And for a similar reason, I have presented the documentary evidence entire in the suit against the late James R. Clement, notwithstanding it greatly increases the expenses of publication, and renders this volume larger than I otherwise would have desired to have given an abstract of the case, and a summary of the evidence would perhaps have given ground to the other party to have charged that it was a partial statement, or that the facts had been garbled. There are many things brought out by the testimony and circumstances alluded to, and the expressions used, that I should have been glad if the mantle of oblivion could have been thrown over them. As it is however, I feel that neither myself nor friends are responsible for this sad affair being dragged before the public and that, to do justice both to the living and to the dead, I have no other alternative left me than to pursue the course which I have. I have forborne to make any farther comment on the unfortunate difficulty between my late son and his wife, and the suit instituted by her against him, than what I deemed absolutely necessary to a proper understanding of the whole matter.

In regard to the prosecution of Capt. Vincent Witcher and his party, for the killing of my sons, I prefer to offer the evidence without any comment from myself. The results of the trial is known to the world. It is proper, also, that all the facts that can be collected should be set forth. Then, and not till then, can a correct opinion be formed by the public. Whether or not the judgment of the majority of the Examining Court in discharging them from further prosecution was correct, it is not proper, perhaps, for me to express my opinion. If justice has not been done, I feel confident that sooner or later, in a higher Tribunal it will be. And I am now willing, with full confidence, to submit the whole matter to the calm and dispassionate judgment of an impartial and intelligent community.

G..W. Clement, Sr.

Near Callands, Pittsylvania Co.
June 4, 1860

There were five justices on the bench at the Examining Court, three of whom were in favor of discharging the accused, and two for sending them on to further trial, as I have been credibly informed.

ORDER FOR SUPPORT
VICTORIA C. CLEMENT vs. JAMES R. CLEMENT

Pittsylvania County, *sct*:

Before me, a Justice of the Peace in & for said County This day personally appeared the within named Victoria C. Clement & John A. Smith & made oath that they verily believe the within Bill to be True - Sworn under my hand, this 30th August, 1859

JOHN D. HALL, J.P.

Pittsylvania County, *sct*:

Before me, a justice of the peace in the County aforesaid this day personally appeared Vincent Witcher and V.O. Witcher, and made oath that they verily believe the facts in the within Bill to be True – Sworn under my hand this 30 Aug 1859

JOHN D. HALL, J.P.

ORDER OF THE COURT

It is ordered that the deft. James R. Clement, pay to the Pltf the sum of two hundred & fifty dollars for her maintenance & to enable her to carry on this suit & the said defendant is hereby inhibited from imposing any restraints whatever on the personal liberty of the Pltf and it is ordered that the defendant deliver to the *pltf* her infant child, Lelia & if the defendant Shall fail on being served with a copy of this order to deliver said child to the Pltf Or to any one authorized by her to receive it, then the Sheriff of Franklin is directed to take the said child into custody *wheresoever* found & to deliver it to the *pltf.* And unless the deft. Shall enter into bond with good security in the penalty of ten thousand dollars before the Clerk of the of the Circuit Court of Franklin, conditioned to have his property real property forthcoming to answer any future order of the Court in the Cause - then the Sheriff of said County is directed to take possession of the estate real & personal, of the deft & to hold it until the further order of the Court.

GEO. H. GILMER, 1st Sept 1859 {Note: the typed transcript reads Augt. 31, 1859}

LAST WILL and TESTAMENT of JAMES R. CLEMENT

Franklin County, Virginia Will Book 11, Page 327

In the name of God amen

I James R. Clement of the County of Franklin and State of Virginia contemplating the end of life from assassination or attack from my enemies such as I experienced at Sandy Level in the *county* of Pittsylvania on the 14th *Inst* but being of sound and disposing mind and memory do make this my last will and testament herby revoking all others.

First I wish and desire that all my just debts burial & funeral expenses be paid. Second, I give and bequeath the whole of my estate real & personal of whatever kind *soever* including my interest in my father''s estate to my daughter Lelia Maud Clement on the following conditions to have and to hold the same forever if she lives to marry, but if she dies before marriage then I wish the whole of my estate to revert back to my next of kin and be distributed *amoung* them according to law. Further I appoint Madison D. Carter of Patrick County & State of Virginia the Guardian of my said child and wish and request him to take my said child and her property and hold the same till she attains the age of Twenty one years or *marrys*. To my Victoria C. Clement I give nothing Having as I confidently believe dishonored my bed left my house & home and used every exertion to ruin me in character and purse. I think she has forfeited all right to Dower in my estate and I wish to exclude her from it altogether. But if she is entitled to Dower I wish to confine her to the lowest limit known to the law.

> Done on the *20* day of September Anno Domini 1859
> James R. Clement

Signed in the presence of
Teste
James L. Rice, George Jameson, Charles R. X Allen, C.C. Murphy.

At a court held for Franklin County at the courthouse the 2nd day of April 1860 This paper purporting to be the last will and Testament of James R. Clement Decd was produced in Court it being proved by the oaths of James L. Rice, Edward C. Murphy and Charles J. Clement that the said paper is wholly in the hand writing of the said James R. Clement Decd and doth order that the said paper be admitted to record as the last will and Testament of the said James R. Clement Decd and on the motion of Charles J. Clement who executed bond with security & made oath a certificate is granted him to obtain letters of administration with the said will annexed.

> Test
> Ro. A. Scott, C.F.C. {Clerk Franklin County}

Order of the Circuit Court of Franklin

AFFIDAVIT OF JAMES R. CLEMENT

September 20, 1859

State   of   Virginia
Franklin County to wit

This day appeared before the undersigned and acting Justice of the Peace in and for the *county* &
State James R Clement of lawful age, and made oath that he is not able according to the best of his
knowledge and belief to attend to his interests in the taking of depositions by the Plaintiff in the
case of Jno A Smith, next friend of Victoria C Clement, against himself without {can't read} to the
records he received on the 14th *Inst* and his general health - that he believes that his interest requires
his presence there, and that he does not believe that any one can by reason of his {can't read}
knowledge of the facts of the Case supply his place
Given under my hand this 20th Sept 1859 Robert
Mitchell J P

DIVORCE DEPOSITIONS
Sandy Level, Pittsylvania County, Virginia
September 21, 1859

DEPOSITION OF S.Y. SHELTON

The deposition of S.Y. Shelton of lawful age, taken at Dickinson"s in the *county* of Franklin, on the 21st day of September, 1859, to be read as evidence in a suit now pending in the Circuit Court of Franklin *county*, between John A. Smith, next friend of Victoria C. Clement, plaintiff, against James R. Clement, defendant. And this deponent after being duly sworn *deposeth* and sayeth:

Question by the plaintiff - Did or not Victoria C. Clement come to your house on the night of the 24th of August last

Answer - I *can not* say that she came to my house on the night of the 24th August last, as I do not remember the date but she did come to my house one night in August last

Question by the same – State as near as you can the time of night she came to your house

Answer - I suppose it was some 9 or 10 *Oclock* but do not know as I had been in bed and asleep

Question by the same. – Did or not any one come with her

Answer - No one that I know of

Question - Was the night dark or otherwise

Answer - The night was very dark

Question by the same - State as well as you can the circumstances under which she came to your house on the night above alluded to, and all that transpired while she *staid* there

Answer - I was waked up by a servant and told that *some one* was calling me, I told the servant that I was not going out to *any body* but to tell them to come to the house by that time the person having kept *hollowing* my family found out who it was I then put on my *cloths* and went out to the blocks or style as quick as I could when I got out to the blocks, she, Mrs Clement, was either kneeling or sitting on the blocks I could not tell which. She asked me to get a horse and my wife & self to go with her to her *mothers.* I told her I could not go but that any of my family might go with her, and if none of them would go that I would send a Negro boy with her. I sent & had a horse caught and she and my wife started when they had gotten some fifteen or twenty steps from the blocks I heard a horse coming apparently as hard as he could run I told them to come back, that James was coming. They turned back and came up to the blocks, got off & went into the house. Mrs. Clement went *up stairs* and told me not to let James come up there. James R. Clement came up about this time and asked me if I had heard from his house *to day.* I told him I had not, he then asked me if I heard from there *to night* I told him I had, he then asked me if Vic was there. I told him that she was *up stairs* he then got up and started towards the open door, and

I told him he could not go up there, he replied that he would see her or kill me one, I then told him he could not come into my house to have any such fusses as that, he then said he was not going to hurt a hair of her head. I then told him he could go *up stairs* and see her and that I would go with him, he started and got about half way up I suppose, he saw some of my girls, I suppose in their night *cloaths,* he turned around and came back and said he would not go up there and sat down by the fire. She then came down on the steps and she and James R. Clement began to quarrel. James R. Clement told her that he supposed that she came down there and told a pretty tale. She replied that she would not have run off if she had not believed that he was going to kill her, he told her that she *knowed* that he was not going to hurt her. She said that she believed that he was fixing to kill her, that he had ordered some hot water put on and that she believed that it was to wash up the blood. *he* told her that was not the reason she ran off. As well as I recollect he then commenced telling her about some Cards which he had found, and said that a certain man had dropped them there for the purpose of giving signs where to meet him. She told him that he was a liar, he said he then had one or two of the cards in his pocket. She told him to draw them out and show them. She said that if he had any cards he had forged them. He told her that he would show them time enough for her good

Question by the same - did she or not tell him that he had ordered his horse well fed that he might be caught and saddled at a moment"s warning

Answer - She did

Question by the Same - did she not tell him that he had been Beating the negroes nearly to death to make them tell upon her that she had been committing adultery with some man or in the woods with some man

Answer - she did

Question by the Same - did she or not tell him that he had driven every negro from the house, and threatened that if they come to any call or outcry that might be made in the house that he would kill them instantly

Answer - I do not recollect that she told him so

Question by the Same - did she or not tell him that he had gone to another room after his weapons that she should see them, and that she should confess her guilt or expect the utmost severity

Answer - She did tell him so if not verbatim in amount

Question - Did or not James R. Clement tell her Victoria C. Clement that he had had a man hired at $5 *pr* week to watch her that he had caught her and gotten her card, and that she had to confess it or she could not live with him *any more*

Answer - I cannot say that he told her so

Question by the Same - did he or not tell her that he had proof of her guilt and that she had to make *acknowligements* or that she could not live with him

Answer - he did

Question by the Same - did he or not tell your daughters to put on their *cloaths* and come down that he would see Vic

Answer - I do not recollect that he did

Question by the Same - You have stated in a former answer in this deposition that she stood upon the stair steps and talked or quarreled with him was the door closed or was it opened

Answer - the door was partially closed but not entirely there was a small space between the shutter and post

Question - did she or not continue to ask or beg you not to let him come *up stairs*

Answer - She said two or three times not to let him come up stains, or don''t let him come up stairs once when he was on the steps

Question - With whom do you live

Answer - I live with *Johnson* Clement

Question by the Same - State the relationship existing between *Johnson* Clement and James R Clement, if any

Answer - They are called brothers

Question - How long have you been living there

Answer - I moved there a few days before Christmas

Question - do you or not and family live in the dwelling-house of *Johnson* Clement

Answer - I and my family *does* live in the dwelling-house of *Johnson* Clement

Question by the Same - is there any bargain or agreement between you and *Johnson* Clement to the effect that you are to live with him another year

Answer - There is an agreement between us to that effect

Question - Was the bargain above alluded to concluded before or since the separation of James R. Clement from his wife

Answer - The bargain was made since the *seperation*

Question - State what Victoria C. Clement told you concerning her leaving and the whipping of the negroes, or said in your presence before the arrival of James R. Clement

Answer - She said that James had beat the negroes mighty nigh to death that the last she heard of *Eleyra*, she just could groan, to make her tell something on her and wanted me to go up there to keep James from killing them. I told her I *want* going, that I would send after Johnson. She said she did not want any more of those rotten-hearted Clements about her. I have already stated in a former answer what occurred at the blocks

Question - Did Victoria C. Clement make no statement or give you no version of the reason why she left that night the house of James R. Clement If she did, state what they were whilst at the blocks or before James R. Clement came up

Answer - I have already answered the question above

Question - State whether or not you saw the girl *Elvira* shortly after this statement of Victoria C. Clement. And, if you did, what she was doing and what appeared to be her condition

Answer - I think I saw her some three or four days afterwards she was walking along with a lap full of peaches on Sunday I could not tell anything was the matter with her as I did not examine her was not very near her, any thirty or forty steps

Question - State whether James R. Clement appeared to be, while conversing with the said Victoria C. at our house, violent in his manner and language, and whether he used say language of threat against her. If he did, state what it was

Answer - I thought when he first came in that he looked somewhat wild, but after conversing awhile appeared pretty much as usual he never made no threats in my hearing

Question - State whether said Victoria C. Clement appeared to be in a passion or not, and whether her language and *behaviour* looked as if she was afraid of James R. Clement while conversing with him

Answer - She talked like she was mad she did not talk like she was afraid of him, though I did not see her while she was on the steps

Question - State if she did not during the conversation she had with him tell him several times to kiss her foot

Answer - She did

Question - State if she did not in the same conversation tell him, James R. Clement, to kiss her back side and bark at the hole

45

Answer - She did

Question - What did James R. Clement say when she told him that she believed he was going to kill her, and that he had warm water put on, etc

Answer - He told her that he had the water put on to wash his feet that she *knowed* that he was not going to kill her

Question - State what James R. Clement said when she told him that he had ordered his horse well fed, that he might be brought and saddled at a moment"s warning

Answer - He said that he had ordered his horse fed but did not say that he wanted him saddled at a moment"s warning that he did not expect to want him that night

Question - State what James R. Clement said when she told him he had gone to another room after his weapons that she should see them and that she should confess her guilt or expect the utmost severity

Answer - To the best of my recollection he said it was not so, or that she *knowed* it was not so I cannot say which

Question - State if James R. Clement did not come down stairs of his own free will and accord, and whether he expressed any wish or made any attempt to go *up stairs* afterwards

Answer - He did come down of his own accord and did not make any attempt to go up again

Question - State whether or not the said James R. Clement did not go away without any attempt to coerce the said Victoria C. home with him

Answer - He did go off without trying to force her to go with him
   SHIRWOOD Y. SHELTON

The further taking of depositions is adjourned till to-morrow morning half past six *oclock*

Thursday morning, forty minutes past seven o"clock, September 22nd 1859. The deponent, S.Y. Shelton, being again called and sworn, pursuant to adjournment, *deposeth* and sayeth:

Question - You said in reply to a former question put to you by the plaintiff, that James R. Clement told Victoria C. Clement he had proof of her guilt, and that she had to confess it, else not live with him *any more*, and expect the utmost severity. Now state if you understood James R. Clement, in that conversation, to tell her that he would use severity and cruelty towards her if she lived with him *any more*

Answer - I do not recollect that he did. I do not recollect that he said anything on that subject

Question - State if the whole conversation of James R. Clement was, or was not, mild and gentlemanly, and if that of Victoria C. Clement was, or was not, violent and abusive

Answer - I never heard two people quarrel that their conversation was mild they both talked loud, and I thought was mad

Question - Did, or did not, you tell R.A. Clement, the Sunday before the first Monday in this month that James R. Clement was perfectly quiet and said nothing out of the way to his wife

Answer - If I stated it then I do not state it now, that I am now upon oath

Question by the Same - State if Victoria C. Clement did not, whilst at your house, abuse James R. Clement and all his friends

Answer - She did all his relations

Question by the Same - State whether or not she continued her abuse of James R. Clement after he had left, and whether her manner was excited or mild

Answer - She kept talking about him, and I believe she was mad

Question - State whether or not you heard *any one*, on the night Victoria C. Clement come to your house, calling the said Victoria C. Clement, and if you did state who it was and what said Victoria C. Clement said about it

Answer - I heard somebody call her, and she said that it was a negro boy called Steve, and that she would answer him to save their lives

Question by the Same - State if James R. Clement did or did not tell you, or some other person in your presence, the same night Victoria C. Clement came to your house, the reason why she left. If he did, state what he said she left for and how

Answer - He said she had got mad and was off without any cause, because he had whipped a Negro boy which her mother had given her. I have not heard him say so but I do not recollect that he said so that night

Question - State whether or not he said that night either to her or you or *any one* else that he insisted on her staying till morning, and that she could take a horse and go if she would go

Answer - he said that he told her to stay all night and that she could have a horse next morning if she would go. I do not recollect whether this was said in the presence of Victoria C. Clement or not

Question - State whether or not James R. Clement further said upon her expressing her determination to go that night, he ordered a horse and she left before he came

47

Answer - If he did I do not recollect it

Question by the Same - State whether or not James R. Clement told either Victoria C. Clement or you or *any one* else that night *any thing* about her squalling and making a great fuss whilst he was whipping the negroes

Answer - he said that night that she was *hollowing* about it

Question - Did you or did you not have a conversation with James R. Clement relative to the manner in which Victoria C. Clement left his house on that night, out of your house

Answer - he said much about it out of doors, that she was in the habit of running out and staying a little while and coming back, and that he thought that she would do the same that night. I do not recollect anything at this time, though he said much

Question by the Same - State whether or not James R. Clement told Victoria C. Clement on the same night that if she was determined to leave him, she could take the child; if he did, state what said Victoria C. said in reply and all about it

Answer - He told my wife in my *presense* that he would send the child down to my house on the next morning. And he told me after he had started out at the fence, that if Mrs. Smith sent after it to let her have it and he told Victoria C. Clements that she might take the child and keep it till it got so that he could raise it if she would then give it back to him she said that she would do no such thing. The Conversation between him and V.C. Clement took place in the house before he left. The child was not sent to my house. Mrs. Smith''s overseer came after the child the next morning. James R. Clement had not sent the child and Mrs Smith''s overseer started up to James R. Clements after it and met him with it and he, James R. Clement as I afterwards understood, carried the child to Ralph A. *Clements*

Question by Same - State how far you live from James R. *Clements* and whether or not you know Victoria C. Clement to have been frequently from home

Answer - I live something like a mile from James R. Clement. I have seen her passing on I suppose once or twice to her mother''s and sometimes for a month or two I did not see her pass at all when I was not at work on the road

Question - State if you ever knew, Victoria C. Clement to pass your house without James R. Clement being with her and if you did how many times and who was with her

Answer - I do not recollect seeing her pass more than once or twice without James R. Clement being with her, and when he was not a Negro girl was with her. I suppose the negro Girl to be some ten or twelve years of age, she might be older or younger

Question by Same - State if you ever knew Victoria C. Clement to go from home without her infant

48

Answer - to my knowledge I never did

Question - Did or did you not on one occasion see James R. Clement pass & *repass* by your house with his infant child in his arms enquiring after Victoria C. Clement

Answer - I saw him passing down to Mrs. *Smiths* with the child on one occasion but did not see him return and he asked me if I had seen Vic pass. I told him I had not this was the Monday or Tuesday evening before the *seperation* on Wednesday

Question - You said in reply to a question put to you by the plaintiff that you lived with Johnston Clement. State whether you live with him as an overseer or otherwise

Answer - I live with Johnston Clement as an overseer

Question - State whether or not Johnston Clement has not been boarding elsewhere ever since you lived with him

Answer - Since February he has been boarding at Mrs. Gilbert"s, coming home sometimes on Saturday or Sunday and sometimes not. He has his clothes washed at home

Question - In the bargain between you and Johnston Clement to live with him next year, was any provision made for his boarding with you

Answer - There was not

Question - Did Johnston Clement or not, tell you that you would have to build a house, and that he would need his own

Answer - He told me that probably I would have to do so

Question - State if Johnston Clement ever expressed to you any dissatisfaction as an overseer before the separation of James R. Clement and wife

Answer - He never did before or since

Question - State if James R. Clement, or Johnston, or any of James R. Clement"s friends, ever attempted, directly or indirectly, to get you to give testimony in their favor contrary to truth

Answer - They never did

Question - State if James R. Clement R.A. Clement and Johnston Clement, in the conversation they had with you about the matter, tell you expressly that they did not wish you to tell *any thing* but the truth

Answer - They did. *Johnson* Clement never said anything about the matter to me but once or twice

Question - State how many times R.A. Clement asked you to give him a statement of the case

Answer - I do not recollect that he ever asked me to give him the particulars more than once

Question - State if Vincent Witcher, the man now taking depositions for Plaintiff and Mary Smith the mother of Victoria C. Clement did come to your house several times since the separation of James R. Clement & wife or not and if they did state whether they were ever there before

Answer - Mrs. Smith came to my house twice since the *sepearation*, once she did not come in the house, the first time she came she asked my wife to go with her to James R. Clement"s after Victoria C. Clement"s *cloths*. Mrs. Smith was also at my house on the night of the *seperation* I having sent for her to come after her daughter which makes three times in all since the very hour of the separation. Vincent Witcher and Oliver Witcher came by my house the day after the separation on their way from James R. *Clements* to Mrs *Smiths* and Vincent Witcher & John A. Smith has been at my house once since, to tell me that they were going to take depositions at Sandy Level, and also to request me to attend as they wished to take my deposition to be read as evidence in this cause, saying it would be more convenient to me there than elsewhere. Mrs. Smith had been at my home once before the *seperation*, Vincent Witcher never, Mrs Smith *stoped* at my house to get out of the rain & *stay* an hour or so

Question - Did or did not Vincent Witcher ask you both times he was at your house questions concerning the testimony you would give and if he did state if he did not on the last occasion tell you how he understood you to have said and ask you if it was not so

Answer - Vincent Witcher asked me some questions but I do not recollect what they were

Question - Did or did he not say that he understood you to say that James R. Clement told Victoria C. Clement that he had a man hired to watch her at so much a week, and that he had caught her in the very act and ask you if it was not so

Answer - I told Vincent Witcher that it might have passed but if so I did not recollect it

Question - State whether or not your wife and daughters were not invited to Mrs Smith"s by Mrs Smith and Vincent Witcher when they were at your house and whether or not Mrs Smith ever sent for them afterwards; and, if so, how often

Answer - I do not know that either of them ever invited my wife and daughters to Mrs *Smiths* I recollect on a Sunday a Negro coming to my house belonging to Mrs Smith saying that Victoria C. Clement had sent for me and my wife

Question by Same - State whether or not your wife & daughter after the separation of James R. Clement & wife did not go to Mrs Smiths and how came they to go there

Answer - I know they said they had been there. I know nothing about it of my own knowledge

Question by the Same - Did or did not Vincent Witcher tell you in one of the conversations he had with you that he could not be surprised if attempts to bribe you were made

Answer - I do not recollect that he did

Question by the Plaintiff - You have already stated that you sent for Mrs Smith to come after her daughter, please state how long after being sent for before she Mrs Smith and her son, *V.O.* {Vincent Oliver} Smith, arrived at your house

Answer - I suppose it was some hour or hour & a half

Question by the Same - Was or not your family and Victoria C. Clement very much alarmed and in tears when they arrived

Answer - Victoria C Clement was pretty much crying all the time she was at my house, would talk some and cry some and *some times* both at the same time, My family had been crying from alarm I suppose, but whether they were crying when Mrs Smith and her son arrived I do not know

Question by the Same - Have you or not any reason for believing that James R. Clement was lurking about your house until after Victoria C. Clement left there. If so, state what those reasons are

Answer - I have no reasons for believing that such was the fact

Question by the same - Did or did not James R. Clement offer you five dollars to walk with him that night

Answer - He did offer me five dollars to go home with him that night

Question by the same - State the reasons which he gave, if any, for offering to hire you to go home with him, and all that he said in relation thereto

Answer - He said that he wanted me to go with him to the hollow tree where they had been dropping their notes that one of them was there then that he wanted me to go and satisfy myself. I told him that it was none of my business and that I was perfectly satisfied about it. He said that it was the first favor which he had ever asked of me, and that if I did not go that it would be the last. I told him that I would come up in the morning if that would do him he replied if I did go that night I need not come. I told him I was not going that night

Question by the same - Please state whether you felt entirely safe in going with him from his conduct and appearance

Answer - I *can not* say that I was afraid to have gone with him, had I wished to have done so

Question by the same - State what was his appearance while he was at your house, particularly when he threatened to kill you if you did not let him go *up stairs*, where his wife was. Was it angry and excited, or was it mild as usual

Answer - He was more angry than usual

Question by the same - Did he or not during his stay at your house, request his wife to return home and live with him

Answer - I do not recollect that he did. I heard her tell him two or three times that she would not live with him

Question by the same - from all which you could gather from the two, did it seem or not, that his visit to your house was to bring about a reconciliation, or was it to abuse her for being too intimate with other men, and to make her confess the fact and apologize for so doing, or make an apology to him

Answer - The next of his talk was about her being too intimate with other men, and about their cards that was very near all the talk between them he accusing and she denying

Question by the same - You have before stated some rough language as coming from her to him. Was that in reply not to his accusations of her being too intimate with other men

Answer - I think it was

Question by the Defendant - State whether or not, you would not be excited should your wife run off from you to a neighboring house, and tell a false tale of an attempt on your part to kill her, and the owner of that house were to refuse your admittance to her

Answer - I would be excited and would be very clear of following her

Question by same - State if you think it anything unreasonable in James R. Clement to follow his wife who had been in the habit of going off and coming back again, leaving home so dark a night and against his *remonstrances*

Answer – It is a thing which I would not do but cannot say that he would regard such a course as unreasonable

Question – You have already stated that Victoria C Clement did not appear while conversing with James R Clement at your house, alarmed but excited and mad. Now state whether or not you mean to say that Victoria C Clement became alarmed after James Clement had left

Answer - I could not see what was to alarm her after he had left more than she was already alarmed after James R. Clement had left

And further this deponent sayeth not - SHIRWOOD Y. SHELTON

52

The foregoing depositions of Shirwood Y. Shelton, *was* taken, sworn to and subscribed before me one of the commissioners in chancery of the Circuit Court of Franklin *county*, at Dickinson''s, in said *county*, on the 21st and 22nd days of September, 1859, agreeable to the caption on the first day, and pursuant to adjournment on the last before named.

Given under my hand as commissioner aforesaid the 22nd day of September, 1859

                  Jas. Petterson Commr

Commissions for taking the deposition $10.00 charged to John A Smith Next friend of V.C. Clement

EXCEPTION BY RALPH A. CLEMENT

September 22, 1859

The defendant by Ralph A. Clement who appeared for him excepts to the whole of the within deposition being used in the Cause because of the inability of the said defendant to be present, and offered his affidavit sworn before me acting justice of the Peace for Franklin County to that effect, and demanded that said affidavit be herewith filed, which is accordingly done. Given under my hand as Comr in Chancery of the Circuit Court of Franklin County the 22nd day of September 1859

                  Jas. Patterson Comr

DEPOSITION OF CHARLES POWELL

The deposition of Charles Powell, taken at Sandy Level, pursuant to notice thereof, on Tuesday the 12th day of September, 1859, to be read as evidence on the trial of a suit now depending and undetermined in the Circuit Court of Franklin *county*, on the chancery side thereof, wherein John A. Smith, as the next friend of Victoria C. Clement, is plaintiff, and James R. Clement, is defendant. Deponent after being sworn saith:

Question - First by the plaintiff. Are you acquainted with Victoria C. Clement

Answer - I have been since her infancy

Question - How near to you was she born and has ever resided

Answer - Not more than two and a half or three miles

Question - What has always been her reputation and standing as a lady of virtue

Answer - I never heard her virtue or ladyship questioned by any one

CROSS QUESTION BY DEFENDANT

Question - Did you never hear, since the marriage of the said Victoria C. Clement with the said James R., that the said Victoria was rude and uncivil to the said James R. If you have, state whether it was in public or private

Objected to by plaintiff and overruled by the *court*

Question 2nd by same - Were you never at the house of James R. Clement whilst the said Victoria C. lived with him If you were, state what was the general conduct of the said James R. Clement towards the said Victoria C., and of the said Victoria C. towards the said James R.

Answer - I have been there two or three times, and so far as my observation went their conduct was kind, each to the other

Question 3 by same - State whether you ever saw the parties in public and whether or not the said Victoria C. appeared to be under any restraint in regard to her acquaintances, male or female

Answer - I have seen them at meeting twice or thrice, and never discovered that he laid any restraint upon her with either male or female

Question 4 by same - Was the general deportment of the said Victoria in public, so far as you have seen it, grave and melancholy, or sprightly and lively

Answer - I never observed anything in her conduct very particularly any way

Question 5 by same - Did you never see her receiving the attention of her friends, both male and female, without any apparent restraint - the said William P. Gilbert of the number

Answer - I have never seen any particular attentions paid to her by any one, and I don"t recollect seeing Buck Gilbert ever speak to her

Question by Plaintiff - At the time to which you allude of having seen the parties at meeting, did you know of any unfriendly relations between the man and his wife so as to call your attention to their conduct

Answer - I did not know of any disagreement between them, but previous to the last time I saw them at meeting I had heard a rumor that there was a disagreement between them

Question by Defendant - State what the rumor was

Answer - I can say no more about it than that I heard that there was a disagreement between them, but did not understand what was the source of {the} disagreement. I did not believe the report when I heard it

And further this deponent saith not

CHARLES POWELL

DEPOSITION OF WILLIS WOODY

The deposition of Willis Woody, taken at the time and place indicated in the caption foregoing.

Deponent being first sworn says:

Question 1st by Pltf - Are you acquainted with Victoria C. Clement

Answer - I was some years ago, but I have never seen her since she was married

Question 2nd by same - How far was she born and raised from your residence

Answer - If she was born where Dr. Smith died, it was not more than two miles. I do not know of my own knowledge where she was born. I knew her when she was very small

Question 3rd by same - What has always been her reputation and standing as a lady of virtue
Answer - She stood very fair as to Character

And further this deponent saith not.

WILLIS WOODY

DEPOSITION OF GEORGE T. BERGER

The deposition of George T. Berger, taken at the time and place indicated in the foregoing caption.

1st Question by Pltf - Are you acquainted with Victoria C. Clement and if so, how long have you been acquainted with her

Answer - I am, and have been acquainted with her for at least ten years. I have resided within one mile of {her} for about seven years previous to her marriage, and about three miles Since her Marriage

2nd by same - What has *allways* been her general character as a lady and a woman of virtue

Answer – As far as I know her Character has been as good as any *Ladys*, whatsoever, as a Lady and a Woman of Virtue

Question by defendant - State whether or not the said Victoria C. Clement was not but a few weeks before marriage with James R. Clement, from an understanding in your family, engaged to your Brother Samuel B. Berger and whether or not you ever heard a report that the said Victoria C. was not attached to the said James R

Overruled by the Court

Question 2 by the same - State whether or not you ever saw the said Victoria C. Clement since her marriage with the said James R. Clement in public company. If you have, state whether you observed any restraint on her part in conversing with and receiving the attention of her friends, male or female

Answer - I have seen her in company frequently since her marriage, and I never saw any restraint on her part

Question 3rd by same - Have you not seen the said Victoria whilst at church and at other places receiving the attention of unmarried men, and apparently enjoying herself since her marriage

Answer - Not that I recollect I have no recollections of any such thing

Question 4th by same - What was the general deportment of the said Victoria C. Clement in company so far as you have observed it since her marriage - grave and melancholy or lively & cheerful

Answer - I have never seen any difference in her deportment since her marriage from what it was before her marriage

Question 5th by same - State what that deportment was – grave and melancholy or lively and cheerful

Answer - Her deportment has ever been since I knew her, lively and cheerful

Question 6th by same - State whether or not the said Victoria C. Clement was, of your own knowledge or from common report, often from home on visits to her friends and in attending public places

Answer - I do not know of my own knowledge. I have heard that she was frequently at her Mother's

Question 7th by same - State whether or not the said Victoria C. Clement was not at all or the most of the public places where it was proper for ladies to be, at which you have been in some 4 or 5 miles from her residence, since her marriage

Answer - I have seen her more frequently at church than *any where* else. I do not recollect that I ever saw her at but one other public place since her marriage, and that was at a show at *Muses* Store, and then in a buggy with her husband starting off. I had not seen her before that day

Question 8 by same - State whether or not there was any other public gatherings in the neighborhood of James R. Clement, at which ladies *was* present, and where you were, after the marriage of the said James R. Clement

Answer - I don't recollect any except those mentioned, except an examination of Godfrey's school, and she was present at the examination

Question by Plaintiff - Did you ever see her at any public place since her marriage without James R. Clement was with her

Answer - I never did

Question by same - When in company, when she was receiving the attention of friends as before stated, where was James R. Clement, close by her or otherwise

Answer - I do not recollect

Question by same - Have you ever known her to make any visits without her husband being with her And, if so, state where and when to the best of your recollection

Answer - I never have to the best of my recollection

Question by Defendant - Was James R. Clement always with her whilst at her Mother's

Answer - I don't know I never saw either of them there since her marriage.

Question by defendant - Did you ever meet her and James R. Clement except at the public places stated above

Answer - Not that I recollect.

Question by the Defendant - Was it the constant habit of James R. Clement when going to church with his wife, to take his seat by her side and remain there till she was ready to return home

Answer - Not that I know of

Question by defendant - Did you never see the said James R. Clement during divine service, or before or after, mixing with the people without his wife while she was at church

Answer - I have

Question by Plaintiff - Have you at any time seen anything peculiar or unusual in the conduct of James R. Clement towards his wife, whilst at church If so, state what it was

Ans - I never have

And farther this deponent saith not

     G.T. Berger

DEPOSITION OF WILLIAM P. GILBERT

The deposition of William P. Gilbert, taken at the time and place indicated in the foregoing caption.

Question by plaintiff - Are you acquainted with Victoria C. Clement

Answer - I am

Quest. 2nd by same - Please state what you know about Victoria C. Clement"s general character as a lady and a woman of virtue also, all you know or believe affecting her character as a lady and a woman of virtue, or in any wise affecting her standing in society

Answer - As far as I am able to know what her general character is, it is that of a lady, and a lady of undoubted virtue. And I know nothing of my own knowledge to the contrary, having been with her a good deal before her marriage and since. I regard her as a lady of virtue, and when in my sight as prudent as ladies generally are

Quest. 3rd by same - When was you last at James R. Clement"s, as near as you can recollect

Answer - between the first and eighth of last January

Quest. 4th by same - Who was there with you and was one of the *outter* doors of the house reported to have been found open the next morning and if anything was said in relation to the opening of said door what was said and who by

Answer. John H. and James C. Witcher were there with me upon that occasion. I went home with James R. Clement upon that occasion at his urgent solicitation and next morning James R. Clement asked me if I had gone out of doors that night, & before or after he asked the question, he asked me if I heard any noise about the house that night. I do not think I can repeat the conversation precisely as it *occured*, but can give the substance, which is as follows: He told me then that Vic *hunched* him in the night and waked him, and asked him if he didn"t hear that noise. I do not recollect whether he said he heard the noise or not. He wished me to speak candidly in reference to my going out that night, and said when I spoke candidly he always believed me. I then assured him that I did not go out that night after I retired, and did not leave my room. He then said that that satisfied him, and said the reason why he wished me to candid about it, was that he thought probably that I might have gone out on a Spree, as he and I had done sometimes previous to this marriage, and he wished to know whether that was the case or not - not that he cared anything about it. He also told me that the door had been found open before of mornings when it was known to have been fastened the night before and also, that they had heard some noise about the house after they had retired, and that his wife was very wakeful, or very easy to wake, and that she was very easily frightened of a night, or was *verry scarry* of a night. I do not recollect which and that when she would hear a noise of a night that she would not call him but hunch him, and ask him if he heard that or to listen. I think both expressions were used. The noise spoken of that night I thought was accounted for when we heard from the two young *Witcher's* that morning, as they said one of them had occasion to get up that night

60

and made some blunders in the dark, which they said made a good deal of noise, and that seemed to relieve Clement"s mind so far as the noise was concerned as I thought at the time. And when myself and the two young *Witcher's* were going to leave Clement, having reasons to believe that I had more money about my person than I was in the habit of carrying, he told me he wanted me to count my money before I left. I told him it was unnecessary, that my money was all right. He said the circumstances of that door being open, he would not be satisfied unless I counted it in his presence before I left

Question 5th by same - Will you please assign the reason why you have not visited his house since the time of your last visit spoken of above

Answer - I suppose I should have visited his house sometime when I did not, had it not been for the condition of his family and before his family got in a condition that I would have visited his house a *Sircumstance* that occurred as I heard between him and one of mother"s negroes, after which I determined not to visit him until we met and had a conversation about the *Sircumstances* to him, and when we did meet somewhere between four and five months since I was at his house last, I was at church, and him and his wife drove up in a buggy. I approached them and spoke as I had usually done, first to his wife as she was facing of me and he had his back to me as I went up. I thought that my speaking to his wife confused her which confused me I then spoke to him in the usual way, and he spoke very coolly. It then occurred to me that his and the negroes difficulty was the cause of his treating me coolly. And I thought that if he was so foolish as to get mad at me for his and the negroes" difficulty, when I thought that he was the *blameable* one, that I would just pass him coolly. And after that when we met we generally said, how are you Jim, and how are you Buck, and shook hands and *past*

Quest 6th by same - Has *any one* been boarding with you lately If so, state who it was, when the board commenced and when it terminated also where the boarder, if any, usually slept

Answer - Charles J. Clement commenced boarding with me some time in last February, and quit not far from the twentieth of last month. We slept up stairs all the time he was boarding there in the same bed with very few exceptions, when there were company there

Question 7th by same - What relation, if any, is Charles J. Clement to James R. Clement

Answer - He is said to be a Brother

Question 8th by same - Had the time for which he set in to board with you expired or not and if not, for what cause did he quit as far as you know

Answer - My understanding from him was that he set in to teach a day school, and that if his school would justify it he would teach the year out, and that he would board with me during the school. The morning before the Night that I afterwards learned that James R *Clements* wife left him Charles J. Clement told me he was going from his school to Mrs. James"s, to stay all night and asked me to come by the schoolhouse and go with him. I answered that I had for some time been thinking that I would go there and stay all night and I thought it was likely I would do so. But went to the shop that evening and was detained there until it was so late I did not do so it was a few days then before C.J. Clement came to my mother"s any more. When he came he called for a settlement which was made, and left without any explanation

Question 9th by same - Have you met with James R. Clement since he and his wife separated before today If so, state the circumstances of the meeting

Answer- I went to Mr. Murphy"s on Sunday morning after I had learned they had separated on Wednesday night before, and found James R. Clement sitting in Murphy"s *poarch* and looked at him intending to speak as I had been speaking. He had his head *sorter* tucked and did not look up. He remained in the *poarch* a few minute*s* then went into the house, after which I saw him no more that day

Question 1st by Defendant - When were you last at James R. Clement"s in company with the two Messrs. Witchers state if you slept in the same room with them or not and if you did not, how were you separated

Answer - I did not sleep in the room with them. We were separated by their being told to go to one room and James R. Clement"s conducting me to another, is my recollection

Question by the defendant - Were not the two rooms in which you and Messrs. Witchers slept, reached by separate stairs and through different passages

Answer - They were

Question 3rd by same - Did not the stairs from the room in which you lodged, run down into the passage to which the door belonged that was reported to have been opened

Answer - I think it did

Question 4th - Were not the stairs that led to the room in which the Messrs. Witchers lodged, on the opposite side of the bed-chamber of the said James R. Clement and could the passage door that was found opened, have been opened by them without going through the chamber

Answer - If my recollection serves me right about the arrangement of the house, they would have had to have gone through the room where Clement and his wife were, or got outside and gone around the house to have got to the door which was purported to have been open that morning neither do I believe that either of them opened that door or was it that night

Question by same - State whether or not, by going out on your last supposition, an outer door would not have had to been opened, and the door purporting to have been opened on the outside

Answer - I would think so

Question by same - State if you did not, when you three were told that there was but one bed in each room, and that you would either have to sleep all three together, or one sleep in a separate

62

room, if you did not volunteer to sleep in the room in which you lodged immediately over the head of said Clement and wife

Answer - My recollection is that Mr. James R. Clement settled that point himself

Question - Have you no recollection of having a dispute among yourselves, as to how you should sleep

Answer - I have no recollection of any. I would not think it at all strange if there was something said between we three as to how we should sleep, from the facts, that we were a great deal together and very intimate, and frequently had unmeaning and nonsensical talk

Question by same - You said that one of the Messers. Witchers said he had occasion to get up in the night and made some fuss by means of a blunder. Please state further, if both of them did not tell you or say in your presence, that they had not come down stairs that night, but sat in the window and eased themselves, or made other shift than coming down

Answer - That's my recollection I thought Mrs. Clement done some cutting up about leaving their receipt where they did, did not seem to be mad but scolded them in rather a jocular way

Question by same - Were you not in the habit of visiting or did you not sometimes visit the said Victoria C. Clement, and find her husband absent and spend some time with her alone

Answer - I never was there that I recollect when Mrs. Clement was there but that Mr. Clement was about home, but not always at the house when I went there, and I am confident I was never there fifteen minutes before he made his appearance

Question by same - Were you not there one whole evening with Victoria C. Clement, when James R. Clement and Bailey Julian were at Naaman Law's till near night

Answer - I went there that evening, it was nearly night when I got there. I found Fletcher Clement there and he escorted me to the house and if him or I either left the room before James R Clement and his guest come in I have no recollection of it

Question by Same - State how large Fletcher Clement was, and also if you did not tell William C. Clement in reply to his question how long have you been here, that you left home directly after dinner and came straight on

Answer - I have no recollection of any such question. I recollect very distinctly that I *didnt* go from home here I came from my *sisters* there. I do not know how large Fletcher Clement was, I believe him to be over Twelve years old at that time

Question by Same - State if you did not often, on sometimes go near to the residence of James R Clement either alone or in Company with another after dark

Answer - Upon one occasion I went not very far from his house with another after dark. I did not go inside of his enclosure was in pursuit of a negro and sent to the cabin to know if it was there and shortly left

And shortly left the *farther* taking of the above deposition.
　　　W.P. GILBERT

Continued to *to morrow* at 9 oclock. A.M.
M.P. *Greers*　　　　　　　C.L. Powell, J.P.
　　　　　　　　　　　　Richard Parker, J.P.

The foregoing Deposition of Wm. P. Gilbert, was This day subscribed as far as gone but was not concluded in consequence of medical advice. That it was imprudent to put the witness under examination the said witness being wounded by a pistol shot. {can't read}. The farther taking of said deposition was postponed by mutual consent of the parties.
Sept 14th 1859
　　　　　　　　　　　C.L.　Powell,　J.P.
　　　　　　　　　　　Richard Parker, J.P.

DEPOSITION OF GEORGE *SAMPSON*

The deposition of George Sampson, of lawful age, taken at the store-house of Washington Dickinson, in the *county* of Franklin, Virginia, on Thursday, the 23rd day of February, 1860, pursuant to notice, to be read as evidence in a certain suit in controversy, now pending and undetermined in the Circuit Court of Franklin *county* on the Chancery side of the Court, in which John A. Smith, next friend of Victoria C. Clement, is plaintiff, and James R. Clement is defendant. The deponent, after having been duly sworn, *deposeth* and saith:

{Editor''s note: it is very obvious from the difference in handwriting that the following questions were answered on paper, not recorded as they were spoken}

Question by Defendant - State if ever you had any conversation with S.Y. Shelton concerning the deposition he gave at this place, in the suit of John A. Smith, next friend of Victoria A. Clement, against James R. Clement, and if you did, state that conversation and all about it

Answer - I heard Mr. Shelton speaking of his deposition. He stated to me that he did not give a right deposition. He said the Mr. Witchers taken him out and told him they had stated things, and some had been stated from his house, and he had to give the same testimony or bad might be the consequences. He said he did not do Mr. Clement justice on that occasion he was *affraid* of the Mr. *Witchers* he said that he did not know how soon they put a ball in him or kill him

Question 2nd by Defendant - State if he said anything about certain looks and frowns he received while giving in his testimony. If he did, what did he say of them

Answer - he said they looked at him very cross at times and *helt thir* hands on *thir* revolvers

Question 3rd by Defendant - State if you ever heard Shelton say anything about giving his deposition again. If you did, what did he say

Answer - As well as I recollect he said he would not go anywhere to have his deposition taken any more

Question 4th - Did he say why he would not give it again If he did, what did, what did he say was the reason

Answer - I don''t recollect

Question 5th - State how long it was after the taking of Shelton''s deposition that you had this conversation with Shelton

Answer - I think it was the second morning afterwards

Question 6 - At what time in the morning was it

Answer - As well as I recollect it was when I went in to breakfast

Question 7th - State if Shelton lived where you were at work, and if he did not, what he came there so soon for in the morning

Answer - if I understood it he lived at *Johnsons* Clement nor *fare* off he came to see me *a bout* cutting Tobacco and *mabe* to grind a Knife

Question 8th - State if you know where Johnston Clement and James R. Clement were at that time, and what was their situation

Answer - They were both over there and James Clement called it his home they both appeared to be wounded

Question 9th - State if you know whether they were so seriously wounded as not to be able to travel about

Answer - They did not appear to me to be able to travel any of consequence

Question 10th - State if you were here when Shelton"s deposition was taken if you were state if Johnston Clement and James R. Clement were here, and if not, why they are not here

Answer - I was here one day and James R. Clement and Johnson Clement *ware* not here and the *reson* why, they said they *ware* not able to get here, *ware* not able to get here {sic}

Question 11th - State who of James R. Clement"s friends were here and if you recollect any effort being made to postpone taking Shelton"s deposition till they, or James R. Clement could get here

Answer - As well as I recollect about it Ralph Clement made a proposal for it to be put off. I don"t know who his friends *ware*

Question 12th - State how many of James R. Clement"s brothers were here

Answer - Ralph Clement and Henry if there *ware* any more I don"t know it

Question 13th - How many of the Witchers and Smiths and relations and connections to the other side did you understand or know to be here

Answer - I don"t know but suppose some *sevel* of the Witchers

Question - State if Oliver Witcher, Addison Witcher, Vincent Witcher, William Witcher, John Poindexter, Sam Swanson, John A. Smith, and *Olover* Smith were here or not

Answer - I saw Dr. Poindexter here I saw Samuel Swanson here, Buck Witcher, Vincent Witcher, *Adeson* Witcher, *Olover* Witcher, John A. Smith and *Olover* Smith

Question - State if you know whether or have any reason to believe that the parties mentioned last were armed or not

Answer - I don't know whether they *ware* or not

CROSS EXAMINED BY COUNSEL FOR PLAINTIFF

Question by said counsel - You have stated in a former answer that S.Y. Shelton told you that he did not give a right deposition in this room in this case that the Mr. Witcher had taken him out and told him that he had stated things and that some things had come from his house. Did he state which of the Witchers had taken him out and when they did so, and did he specify what the things were that they told him

Answer - If I recollect right that Oliver Witcher was one of them, and the Witchers they took him out the same day, before he give his deposition. I don't recollect he said the things was, he told him

Question - Who did Shelton come with on the day that he gave his deposition

Answer - I don't know.

Question - Did you see any attempt on the part of any of the Witchers Smiths or Swansons, mentioned by you as having been present, to bully or brow beat Shelton during the time he was giving his deposition Did you hear any of them threaten him - or see them look menacingly at him during said time

Answer - no I don't know that I did

Question by same - Did not Vincent Witcher conduct the examination of the witnesses for the plaintiff Did you see any of the other Witchers, Smith or Swanson take part in the said examination or propound any question to him

Answer - As well as I recollect Vincent Witcher asks the questions, and as well as I recollect, some of the other Witchers whispered to him sometimes

{Question} By Same - Did any of them, except Vincent Witcher, say anything to Shelton during said time Did you come there that day at the request of *any body* If so who requested you to come

Answer - I don't recollect that they did. I proposed to come up in the presence of the Defendant and his father *Doct* Clement and James proposed to lend me a horse, and *Doct.* Said he *wist* I would it was a Rainy Time that I could not do anything else

{Question} By Same Did any persons furnish you with weapons or send weapons by you If any, state who they were

Ansr - no they did not
GEORGE *SAMSON*

The above continued until *to morrow* ten *oclock* the 23rd February, 1860

Question by Defendant - You said in reply to a question asked you by Plaintiff, that you did not see any attempt in the part of the Witchers & others to bully and *brow beat* Shelton whllst on examination. State if you were present and looking on all the time said deposition was being taken, and if your mind was particularly called to their conduct towards Shelton on that day

Answer - I *cant* say that I was present all the time *some times* in and *some times* out

Question by Same - State if you did not hear R. A. Clement tell Shelton in open court, while he was on examination, not to address himself to Vincent Witcher but to the court

Objection by the *plaff council* {Editor"s note: this objection does not appear on the document on the microfilm but was found in Dr. Clement"s book}

Answer - I think I heard you tell him something to that amount

Question by Same - State if you did not hear R.A. Clement complain to the court while Shelton"s deposition was being taken, that answers were dictated to Shelton, or something to that amount and if some misunderstanding between the court and Clement did not take place on that amount

Answer - he and the magistrate had some words about it I don"t recollect the words exactly

Question by Same - You have stated that you remarked on the day that Shelton"s deposition was taken at James R. Clements that if you had a horse you could go up and hear it State if you did not also add, and stay all night at home as you could do nothing else

Answer - Yes, I did go home and stay all night and went to Mr. Clement"s next morning

Question by Same - You have stated that Dr. Clement, the father of James R. Clement, said when you asked for the horse, that he wished you would go. Now state why he said he wanted you to go

Answer - The old *Doct* said if Ralph should happen to get shot or anything of that sort if I would take care of him or let him know

Question by Same - State if you were at James R. Clements on the day James & Johnston Clement were said to have been shot at Sandy Level and, if you were, if said Dr. Clement asked you to go there any time during the day and if he did, say what for

Answer - Yes, I was there on the day they was said to have been shot at work and David Williams came and told me that James Clement said he wanted me to fetch him his buggy to fetch him home. Then I started down there some and the old *Doct* and William and met them fetching them home in a wagon when we met them the old Doctor got me and William to go on to see what had become of Ralph and we met him coming and we turned back

Question by Same - Attempts have been made to learn through you whether or not you were not asked to come here when Shelton"s deposition was taken to take part for the defendant, etc. Now state if James R. Clement, or any of his friends ever attempted to get you to take part in said Controversy in any way whatever or ever asked you to do anything in relation thereto of a dishonorable character

Answer - no none of you never did only the old *Doct* got me to come up here as I stated before

All the questions propounded by the deft. to the witness in his reexamination are objected to by the *plt*.
    GEORGE *SAMSON*

The foregoing Deposition Subscribed and sworn to before me the date before will show
    ROBERT MITCHELL, J.P.

DEPOSITION OF EDNEY SHELTON

The deposition of Mrs Edney Shelton, of lawful age, taken at the Store House of Washington Dickinson, in the *county* of Franklin and State of Virginia, pursuant to notice and according to law, on the 24th day of February, 1860, to be read as evidence in a certain suit now pending and undetermined in the Circuit Court of Franklin *county* on the Chancery side of said Court, in which John A. Smith, next friend of Victoria C. Clement, is Plaintiff, and James R. Clement, is defendant. After being duly sworn the deponent *deposeth* and saith:

Question by Defendant - State if Victoria C. Clement wife of James R. Clement came to your home on the night she left her husband and if she did, state what cause she assigned for leaving her husband whilst there as far as you recollect

Answer - She came to our house that night she left Mr. Clement she came to the blocks that night she said she ran off while he was *whiping* his negroes near the stable. Mr. Shelton asked what he was whipping them for, and she said that he came home Dead Drunk. He asked ware she *ware* going to she said she had started to Mares {mother's}. She then asked me and him my husband to go with her. I then told her I would not go with her I was afraid. She said to me go with me *miss* Shelton I'm not *a fraid* of him he is at home Drunk he was so Drunk that he could not walk across the floor *strait*

Question by Same - State if you recollect whether she said anything about what James R. Clement would do if he were to come after her and she were to go home with him. If you remember *any thing*, state what she said about it

Answer - She said if James Clement had overtaken her - he would if I had went back with him he would have been one of the best *creshurs* I ever saw

Question by Same - Where did you have this talk with her

Answer - I had them between the blocks and the house

Question by Same - How long did you and her stay at the blocks talking before going in the house

Answer - I *recond* we stayed *thare* fifteen *minits*

Question by Same - State if you heard any one calling Mrs Clements at or in the direction of James R. Clements that night if you did *say where* you were when you heard it

Answer - As we went from the blocks to the house she heard them calling of her. She spoke and said she would not answer to save *thier* life. I have heard it

Question by Same - State if Mrs Clement told a second tale about her running away from her husband if she did, tell what it was

Answer - She told that she ran off while Mr. *Clements* had gone in the room to hunt his B*owing* Knives & weapons he had moved Them from *whare* he had *usual* kept them.

Question - State if James R. Clement came to your house that night

Answer - Yes, he came *thare* he asked if Victory was *thare*

Question - Was James R. Clement drunk

Answer - I don't know a drunken man when I see him without he is falling about if he was drunk I could not tell it

Question - State what he said he came for

Answer - he said he was hunting Victory

Question - Did he see her

Answer - I *recond* he Did, I don't know he started up stairs and turned back.

Question by Same - State why he turned back

Answer - I don't know

Question - State what he said he came down for

Answer - he said my daughter was not *dress* and he would not go any *farther*

Question - State if James R. Clement saw her any more that night after he came down

Answer - I *cant* tell whether he saw her or not he was talking her on the stair steps above the stair door

Question by Same - State why she came down that far

Answer - She was talking or *quarling* as hard as she could she wanted to get as *ner* him as she could I *recond* that's what she wanted to come on the steps for

Question by Same - State whether or not you heard or recollect *any thing* said by them to each other that night, and what it was

Answer - I don't recollect James Clement said, Vick when I married you I loved you he said to her that you have it in your power to take the last cent that *Im* worth You poor she said {can't read} not a Dime you have got to save your life

Question by Same - State what James R. Clement's reply to her was

71

Answer - As well as I recollect he said very well Vick or *Verry* good Vick or one of them words

Question by Same - State if either party called the other a liar, and if either did, who it was

Answer - I don''t recollect of any one in Talking Vick *tould* me to come up stairs *ware* she was and not stay *thare lisenging* to James'' lies to {can''t read}

Question by Same - State whether or not you heard Mrs Clement tell James R Clement to kiss her foot

Answer – She said so

Question by Same - Did you or not hear Mrs Clement use obscene and vulgar language to her husband that night

Answer - I heard some

Question by Same - State if James R. Clement said anything unkind or harsh to her whilst at your house that night

Answer - I did not hear *any thing* unkind I was not in the house all the time

Question by Same - State if James R. Clement told her she could have a horse or not, if she would go to her mother''s that night

Answer - he told her she could have a horse that night, if nothing else would do her but to go to her mars {mother''s} that night he told young Shelton the horse had to come back that night and be put up

Question by Same - State what James R. Clement said to his wife about her taking the baby

Answer - He said would she take it and keep it two years and she said she would not take it and keep it that way she said if she could not take the child and keep it *always* she did not want it then

Question by Same - State whether or not Mrs Smith the mother of Mrs. Clement came to your house that night after her daughter. If she did, state what you heard her tell her daughter about leaving her husband

Answer - Miss Smith came there that night after Vick. Vick said mare {mother} I came all the way Down here by *my self*. Miss Smith said if you had *lisen* to me you would have left him long ago. She said *mare* I thought I could live with him

Question by Same - did you or not hear Mrs. Smith say that night that Vic had married somebody she thought herself above

Answer - Miss Smith said Vick you married *soome body* that you was too good for you thought *your Self* above them

Question by Same - How was Mrs Clement dressed on the night she came to your house

Answer – She was Dress in all her cloths she wore that days *secon* all to her Bonnet & shawl and gloves she had on her Bonnet and gloves that night

CROSS EXAMINATION BY THE PLAINTIFF

Question - Have you ever made the foregoing statements before *To day* If so state when as near as you can recollect and to whom

Answer - no I never had only to my own family as I recollect I may *of talk* about it I
 Have talked about it the day after they parted. I *recond* I Talk about it the next week {can't read}

{Question} - You stated in answer to defendant's question that you heard Victoria C. Clement some vulgar and obscene language to James R. Clement, State what that language was

Answer - she told James R. Clement to kiss her foot and to kiss her Back side or *any where* else the balance I *aint* a *goint* to say.

{Question} - Have you never stated to any person or persons that you did not hear Victoria C. Clement use the vulgar and obscene language given above, but that James R. Clement said she should do so

Answer - No sir, I never stated so that last on earth unto no living soul

Question - State where and upon whose premises you were living at the time of the Depositions between James R. Clement and Victoria C. Clement, where you have resided since and where you reside now

Answer - We lived at *Johnson* Clement and we live there yet

Question - What relationship do you understand to exist between the said *Johnson* Clement and James R. Clement

Answer - They are said to be Brothers

Question - Did you or not go to Mary A. Smith's the day after the separation between said James R. Clement and Victoria C. Clement, and then and there profess to make a full statement of all that you know in reference to their separation and especially what passed at your house

Answer - I was *theare* the next day and made no true state of what was said between James Clement and Victory

{Question} - Were you not at the time mentioned in the *preceeding* question cautioned by Vincent Witcher to make no statement that was not true as you might be called upon as a witness

Answer - I don"t recollect any of it but I know I told him that I did not want to be in any scrape having *any thing* to do with it

Question by defendant - How came {you} to go to Mrs Smiths the day after James R. Clement"s and wife"s deposition {Note: Dr. Clement"s book reads: separated}

Answer - Miss Smith *toold* me to come to her house the next day. She said something about her pare {father}. She was going to send for her pare {father}.

Question by Same - State if you heard *any thing* said by Victoria C. Clement & Mrs Smith whilst there, about Victoria going home, if you did, what was it

Answer - Victoria said something about going home, and her mare {mother} said you look like going. She said O mare {mother}, it looks like I must go

Question by Same - State if Mrs Smith ever asked you afterwards to come and see her, and if she ever afterwards come to see you

Answer - She and Victory was once there afterwards but I have not been there *sence* she asked me Several times to come to see her

Question by Same - State if you were not *summoned* to give your deposition here with your husband; if you were why did you not come

Answer - John A. Smith told my husband that thare *ware* no notice said his grand pare said you need not come here unless there *weare* a notice sent to me the night before that"s *what's* I heard

Question by Same - Have you been much excited & alarmed *to day*

Answer - I had been nothing else if I had known I would not *shown* my face here today

{Question} - Did you or not in speaking of the conversation between said James R. Clement and Victoria C. Clement say that you heard James R. Clement say something about having employed a man to watch said Victoria C. and if so, what was it

Answer - no sir I did not hear any thing of that said. No I never said any such Thing
      her
   EDNEY X SHELTON
   Mark

The above Deposition continued until *to morrow*, 10 *OC A.M.*
   ROBERT MITCHELL, J.P.

{Question} - The day after the separation between James R. Clement and Victoria C. Clement did you or not at Mary A Smith"s say that the said Victoria C. was so overcome by fatigue and alarm when you want out to the fence where she was that she fainted or fell down on the blocks and lay some time before she could utter a word and did you not repeat the same thing on the following day to Vincent Witcher and Vincent O. Witcher

Answer - No sir I never repeated no *shuch* thing and never made use of so *shuch* language

{Question} - Were you and your husband both in each other"s presence requested by Vincent Witcher to state *every thing* in reference to said separation within your knowledge and occurring at your house, and informed you would be called on as witnesses and did you not say you were willing to swear to the statement then made by you

Answer - I don"t recollect. I can"t answer that

{Question} - Did you or not at the times mentioned in the *preceeding* questions state that James R. Clement"s language and looks on the night he and his wife were at your house, were so wild and threatening that it greatly alarmed you and that he, the said James R. Clement, threatened to kill your husband, if he did not let him go *up stairs* where Victoria was

Answer - I don"t recollect of ever stating that to Capt. Witcher I *recon* my recollection is as good as his

{Question} - Did you or not at the Times alluded to say that James R. Clement said he had the proofs of Victoria"s adulterous habits with other men and that she should make acknowledgments or never live with him again

Answer - no sir never made use of no such language I never heard him make use of no such language

{Question} - Did you not also state that you had started to carry Victoria to her mother"s and after you had got on the horse you heard a horse coming as hard as it could run, and that you both jumped down and run into the house and Victoria run up the stairs and begged Mr. Shelton not to let James R. Clement go where she was

Answer - yes sir I did

{Question} - Did you not state that after getting off the horse you started a negro boy on the same horse and told him to ride fast as he could after Mrs Mary A. Smith

Answer - Well, I don"t know what I said to him he went after Miss Smith

{Question} - Did you not stat that James R. Clement offered your husband five dollars to go with him to a hollow tree where he, the said James R. Clement, said some of Victoria"s cards or letters were and when your husband refused to go, that he then offered him five dollars to go with him as far as the branch

Answer - I don't think I stated it part of it he made of I *recon* to my husband

{Question} - did you or not at the times alluded to in the foregoing questions or at any other time state that you feared or thought he the said James R. Clement, intended to kill your husband and then return and kill Victoria, but he was afraid to do so then because Mr Shelton's rifle was sitting by

Answer - no sir I made no such statement to *no boddy*

Question by defendant - You stated that you never told any one what you swore to on yesterday. Do you mean that you never told all you swore to, or that you told only a part of what happened at your house

Answer - That's what I meant, I meant I told a part of what *hapen thare*

Question - State whether or not you meant, when you said on yesterday in reply to the question, have you told what you swore to in your deposition to anybody and, if you did tell them to anybody, who you told them to in your deposition to anybody, or only that you had told some things that happened at your house the night Mrs. Clement left her husband and came there

Answer - I have told some things, but I've never all

Question - You stated yesterday, that when Mrs. Clement told her mother that she must go home that her mother said she should not, or something to that *amount*. State whether or not Vincent Witcher was present and if he was, what he said about it

Answer to the foregoing question - *Vict* said something about what she was going to do when she went home and her mare {mother} said you look like going home. She said O mare it looks like I must go back. Capt. Witcher said this is your home Vick He was lying on the bed and said you are not dependent upon James Clement for a home

Question by same - You stated that you went to Mrs. Smith's at the earnest request of Mrs. Smith. State whether she ever invited you before that night

Answer - no sir she never had

Question by Same - State if Mrs Smith ever invited you since that time and how often. Also, how she told you to do when you were coming to her house

Answer - She has invited me *senc* several times and told me when I started to her house to tell them at home I had started to some neighbor's house and come to her house

Question by Same - How were you treated when you were at Mrs. Smith's

Answer - first rate cuts of *rost* chicken and drank of the best

Question - State whether or not the same objection had been made by Capt. Witcher before dinner, that was made after dinner

Answer - If it was made I did not hear it

Question - Were you or not in the room at the time when the magistrate adjourned the taking of depositions for the parties to get dinner

Answer - I was in there at the time they left, but did not know their business

Question - State if you know how long Captain Witcher and his party were absent from the room where the depositions were taking

Answer - I don"t – I can"t specify any length of time

Question - State who come with Captain Witcher when he came back to the room to commence taking depositions

Answer - I do not know

Question - State whether Capt. Witcher repeated the remark, that, if you, the witness, was turned over to the opposite party until Monday, you would be tampered

Answer - He stated it once, and then repeated it

Question - When Capt. Witcher first made the remark, what did Ralph Clement do and say

Answer - He *ris* up from his chair and said that she would not be left in the hands of the opposite party said he, "you may take her and put her in jail or anywhere else you please"

Question - When Ralph Clement got up, where was Capt. Witcher, and what did he do and say

Answer - He was sitting in a chair on the opposite side of the fire-place from where he, Ralph Clement, was sitting. As Ralph Clement sat down Capt. Witcher arose up out of his chair and put his hand in his bosom and stepped a step or two, advancing towards him, and drew his pistol out and fired it over my head

Question - Did you distinctly see some person holding Ralph Clement

Answer - I did

Question - Do you know that the person who had hold of Ralph Clement, took hold of him before the first fire

Answer - He did not take hold of him until after the first fire

Question - Was there any firing in the direction, or near Ralph Clement, whilst the person was holding him

Answer - There was

Question - State if you know how many persons were killed, and *who*

Answer - Three persons were killed, James Clement, William Clement and Ralph Clement was not dead when I left the room, but suppose that he died in a very few minutes after I left the room

CROSS EXAMINATION

Question by the *defence* - When Vincent Witcher asked for a continuance of the taking of depositions, and spoke about picking the witness, to whom di d he address himself

Answer - To Ralph Clement, as I suppose

Question - Why do you suppose

Answer - No person else spoke to him at the time, and I should suppose that it was to Ralph Clement that he was speaking

Question - Did not Ralph Clement reply instantly upon Vincent Witcher making the above request

Answer - Immediately

Question - Was your face turned to Vincent Witcher

Answer - It was

Question - Were you not standing between Ralph Clement and Vincent Witcher

Answer - I was sitting down in a chair between Ralph Clement and Capt. Witcher

Question - Did you see to whom Vincent Witcher looked when he made the above request

Answer - I did not.

Question - Did not Vincent Witcher say to the magistrate, about the time of making said request, that though the magistrate had refused before dinner, to continue the case until Monday, that h had a right to reconsider and change his opinion

Answer - If he did, I don''t recollect it

Question - Did the magistrate say anything at that time

Answer - I don't recollect that he did

Question - Do you have a distinct recollection of what happened on the occasion

Answer - Altogether, I have not. I recollect some things but not all

Question - Who was in the room at the time

Answer - They were pretty much all strangers to me. I did not turn around to look back to see who was in the room I know but two or three gentlemen in the room, Capt. Witcher and the magistrate, I don't recollect his name, and Ralph Clement. I know no one else I expect if I had turned round to look I should have known some other persons

Question - Were there any persons on the bed at the time Vincent Witcher drew his pistol

Answer - I did not notice

Question - Was Vincent Witcher's chair leaning against the bed

Answer - His chair was by the side of the bed, with the back to the bed and against it, and the side of the chair by the side of the wall

Question - When dinner was ready did not the parties on both sides leave the store

Answer - I do not know whether all of them left it or not at the time

Question - When Capt. Witcher made the remark and repeated it about picking, etc., what did Ralph Clement say I mean between the making and repeating the remark

Answer - He said she would not be left in the hands of one of the opposite parties that he had no objections to my being put in jail or anywhere else, he did not care where they put me

Question - Did you know James Clement and William Clement well

Answer - Yes, if I had seen their face

Question - Did you see anything after you got under the writing desk

Answer - Nothing more than Ralph Clement and the gentleman that had hold of him, from about their waist down

Question - Did you not state to George Finney after the shooting that you did not know how it commenced

Answer - No, I did not

Question - Whose witness were you at the taking of the deposition

Answer - James Clement"s

Question - Where were you living at the time

Answer - I was living in the house with my sister, on the land of Ralph Clement.

Question - Was not your sister"s husband Ralph Clement"s overseer

Answer - Yes, he was

Question - How far did you live from Ralph Clement"s house

Answer - I could not be positive about the distance - a very little way - all in sight

Question - How did you get to the place of taking depositions that day

Answer - I rode one of Ralph Clement"s horses

Question - What was the manner of Vincent Witcher when he asked you for a continuance and insisted upon, and stated his reasons for it

Answer - He did not speak as though he was very angry, though his language was not as pleasant as it might have been, speaking in common language

Question - Did you have on your bonnet at the time

Answer - I did.

Question - From the shape of your bonnet, could you see anything that was not directly before your face

Answer - Certainly, I could see a little towards each side

Question - What was the manner of Ralph Clement is replying to Vincent Witcher

Answer - He spoke like he was a little short not as mild as I had heard, but not loud

Question - Did Ralph Clement draw any weapon before or after you went under the desk

Answer - No, none that I know of

Question - Did he leave home with weapons

Answer - I do not know whether he did or did not

82

Question - When Vincent Witcher was rising from his seat, drawing and advancing a step or two to Ralph Clement, what was Ralph Clement doing

Answer - He was setting in his chair doing nothing

Question - In any part of that day, did you hear Ralph Clement say that he expected a difficulty with the Witchers or their friends
Answer - No, I did not

Question - Did you hear the same any short time before that day

Answer - No I did not

EXAMINATION RESUMED IN CHIEF

Question by attorney for prosecution - Do you know whether Capt. Witcher"s chair was leaning back against the bed, or was simply *setting* against the bed

Answer - It was simply *setting* against the bed.

Question - How long do you suppose it was after Capt. Witcher arose from his seat before he fired

Answer - I can"t exactly tell you, but a short space of time as soon as he could advance a step

Question - State anything you may have said to George Finney about the shooting

Answer - I have no recollection of saying anything to George Finney particular about it. He was there at Ralph Clement"s talking to my sister about it. I had but very little conversation with him about it. I think to the best of my recollection, that I asked him if he knew who done the first firing, and I won"t be positive whether he saw it, or said some person told him that it was John Anthony Smith done the first firing

Question - Have you not had and heard very many conversations upon the subject since the shooting, and can you remember the particulars of many of them

Answer - I have heard several, and cannot remember the particulars of many of them

Question - Are you in the habit of wearing bonnets that blindfold you

Answer - No I *ant*

And further this deponent sayeth not.

ELIZABETH W. her X mark BENNETT

DEPOSITION OF ROBERT MITCHELL

Robert Mitchell being called and sworn, says:

On Thursday last, James Clement came to my house and requested me to come to Dickinson"s to take depositions as a justice. I came and commenced taking the deposition of Mrs. Shelton. I did not get through with her deposition adjourned over until next day, 10 o"clock, when her deposition was completed. After closing Mrs. Shelton"s deposition on Saturday about one o"clock, Vincent Witcher asked to have the taking of depositions postponed until Monday, as he did not believe that there would be any chance to get through with them that day that he wished to go home that he lived some fifteen miles. Ralph Clement objected to it said he had a female witness there and insisted on going on and taking her deposition. I decided to go on. There was a conversation commenced between Capt. Witcher and Ralph Clement about that time, which I did not consider there was any malice about more than common. I *ris* up out my chair summoning in my mind, the oath to administer to the witness. I heard the report of a pistol or gun, and from that it continued mighty fast. In a minute or so, there was a heap of fog or smoke, looking towards the door that leads out of that room into the store, I saw Mr. Samuel Swanson striking with a stick left that room and went into the store. I then went out and commanded the crowd to take charge of *them* men. In making my statement in regard to taking the depositions, alluded to, I erred in saying that I commenced taking Mrs. Shelton"s deposition. I commenced with George Sampson and the first day and part of the next was consumed in taking his deposition

Question by counsel for prosecution. When Capt. Witcher, on Saturday, at one o"clock, moved to continue the taking of depositions until Monday, and you decided to proceed with taking the depositions that day, did you proceed forthwith at that time to administer the oath to Miss Elizabeth Bennett

Answer - No I then said they could have a recess of thirty minutes for dinner when the recess was taken I do not recollect that I was asked for it

Question - When re-assembling after dinner, did Capt. Witcher make another motion to the same effect

Answer - I have no recollection that he did

Question - Did you have the notice before you at the time which had been given to take the deposition

Answer - I had the notice at the commencement

Question - Was it stated in that notice that the depositions were to be taken between the rising and setting of the sun on that day

Answer - From an examination of the notice, the depositions were to be taken between the rising and setting of the sun on that day

Question - When the motion was made for the continuance of the taking of the depositions what do you suppose was the time of day

Answer - I think about one o'clock

Question - Why did you decline to adjourn the taking of the depositions

Answer - Because the parties were there and seemed to be ready and Ralph Clement said that there was a female witness

Question - When Ralph Clement made that remark about the female witness, what did Capt. Witcher say in reply

Answer - I do not recollect

Question - Did Capt. Witcher make any reply either to you or Ralph Clement, in consequence of Clement having a female witness here

Answer - If he did I have not recollection of it

Question - Did Capt. Witcher consent to the adjournment, or object to it

Answer - Capt. Witcher made the request for the adjournment

Question - Did Capt. Witcher make the request for the adjournment before the recess for dinner

Answer - He did

Question - Did you overrule Capt. Witcher's proposition before the recess for an adjournment

Answer - I did

Question - Did Capt. Witcher leave the counting-room when the recess was allowed

Answer - I think he did

Question - Who left in company with him

Answer - I do not know

Question - Did Capt. Witcher return to the counting-room after the recess, about the time that you commenced the taking of the depositions

Answer - Capt. Witcher was in the room at the time I was about to commence the taking of the depositions of Elizabeth Bennett

Question - Was Vincent O. Smith, John A. Smith, Samuel Swanson, and Addison Witcher and James Witcher, or any of them in the room, at the time you were about commencing to take the deposition of Elizabeth Bennett

Answer - I do not know. I have stated that I saw Samuel Swanson in the room after the affray commenced, striking with a stick

Question - After the recess, when you were about to administer the oath to Elizabeth Bennett, did Capt. Witcher renew his motion to postpone, after you had overruled the same before the recess

Answer - I do not recollect

Question - Do you remember any remark that Ralph Clement made before the firing began

Answer - I have stated that Capt. Witcher and Ralph Clement were talking, and my attention being drawn in another direction, I cannot say what either of them said

Question - In what part of the room did the report of the first fire seem to you to be

Answer - I cannot say

Question - How long had the firing been going on when you saw Samuel Swanson striking with the stick

Answer – I don't know as I was very much excited

Question by same – In what part of the room was he Swanson striking with the stick

Answer - It was near the door leading out of the counting-room into the store

Question - Do you remember any remark that Ralph Clement made at the time you were about to commence taking the deposition of Elizabeth Bennett

Answer - I do not

Question - Did the person to whom he was giving the blows with the stick fire at him

Answer - If he did, I don't know it

Question - Did you see anybody fall

Answer - I did not

Question - Who were killed and how many

Answer - Ralph A. Clement, James R. Clement and William Clement. When I went out of the house and came back again James R. and William Clement were lying dead on the floor but Ralph A. Clement was not quite dead but died shortly afterwards

Question - In going out did you discover any dead bodies if so, state in what part of the room they laid

Answer - I got over some person lying on the floor I don't know whether they were dead or not the person or body was lying about the foot of the bed with the head towards the post office, which was the only person I saw lying on the floor

Question - Where was Miss Bennett, whose deposition you were about to take at the time the firing began

Answer - She was on the other side of the table from where I stood

Question - Was she sitting or standing

Answer - I do not recollect

Question - Do you know what became of her during the firing

Answer - She crawled under the desk

Question - Did you see Ralph Clement during the firing

Answer - Not as I recollect of

Question - Did you observe Capt. Witcher during the firing

Answer - Not as I recollect

Question - After the firing was over, did you see anybody leave the counting-room with weapons of any kind upon their persons or in their hands

Answer - No

Question - Did you hear any man say he had been in the fight, or had taken any part in any way in it

Answer - I went out in the porch and summoned the crowd to come and take charge of *them* men. In this time, Capt. Witcher or Vincent Witcher come to the door and remarked that I need not be afraid, that there *wan't* a man in there that was *a guine* to run that they *want* running stock. I never heard any man say that he had taken part in the fight. The above is all I heard Capt. Witcher say on the subject. He came to the door that leads from the counting room into the porch, as well as I recollect

Question - Was there not a large quantity of blood upon the floor

Answer - There was

Question - To the best of your recollection or impression, how many shots were fired

Answer - Without knowing, I would suppose some eighteen or twenty. I did not count the balls in the bodies or in the walls

CROSS EXAMINATION BY THE *DEFENCE*

Question - When Vincent Witcher made the motion for the adjournment before the recess, did he not address himself to you as the court

Answer - He did

Question - Who was conducting the examination for the plaintiff

Answer - I think it was Addison Witcher

Question - From the time of commencing the said deposition, up to the time of the recess, was not the manner of the said Addison and Vincent Witcher perfectly courteous and polite to the opposite party, to the suit and his agents

Answer - I thought so

Question - When the motion for the continuance before the recess was made, did not Vincent Witcher and Addison Witcher politely acquiesce in the decision you made

Answer - I think they did

Question - Do you remember on assembling after the recess, while the parties were present to proceed with the deposition, Vincent Witcher addressing himself to you, stated that you had the right to reconsider the decision you had made, and still to grant the continuance till Monday

Answer - I have no recollection of it

Question - Do you remember Vincent Witcher stating after the recess, anything about the witness having to remain in the hands of the opposite party until Monday, unless they then continued the taking of depositions

Answer - I recollect hearing Vincent Witcher say something about the witness being in the hands of the opposite party, but do not recollect what it was my attention about that time having been called to the qualifying of the witness

Question - Did you hear Ralph Clement give the lie to Vincent at any time during the day

Answer - If I did, I have no recollection of it

Question - Did you see Vincent Witcher draw his pistol and advance upon Ralph Clement

Answer - I did not see a pistol in the house at that time, nor did not see him advance nor did I see him at all at that time as I remember

Question - State who was on the bed

Answer - I cannot

Question - Were you not between the table on which the depositions were to be taken, with your back to a small window on the right of the fire-place

Answer - My back was to the jam, the table before me, a small window to my left, right over the desk on the right side of the fire-place that was my position when I got up to swear the witness

Question - Where was Ralph A. Clement at that time

Answer - He was on my left sitting by the table

Question - Where was Addison Witcher

Answer - I have no recollection

Question - Who was on your right at the table

Answer - If there was any person I don"t know. I do not recollect whether Miss Bennett was on the right of the table or at the front of it

Question - Which of the Clements were in the room at the commencement of the firing, and in what part of the room were they

Answer - I have no recollection of but one Clement being in the room

Question - Where were you through the shooting

Answer - I was standing against the jam betwixt the fire-place and desk. If there was any shooting done after I left the room I do not recollect it but do not pretend to say there was not

Question - From the agitation occasioned by the occurrence, can you rely on yourself to give a correct statement of what occurred

Answer - I have given a correct statement of facts so far as I have gone, and can rely on my statement so far as I have gone. I was excited, and don"t pretend to say that there was *occurrances* took place that I don't know anything about at this time that the answers I have sworn to I have a recollection of

Question - State exactly how far you had *proceed* towards swearing Miss Bennett when the firing began

Answer - I had got up out of my chair and was standing up with the book in my hands. I do not recollect whether Miss Bennett had put her hand on the book or not

Question - Was she near enough to reach the book

Answer - She was

EXAMINATION IN CHIEF RESUMED

Question by counsel for prosecution - From the beginning to the end of the taking of the depositions, was not the conduct of James Clement, and Ralph Clement, and William Clement, entirely polite to the opposite party as far as you saw

Answer - I think so

CROSS EXAMINATION RESUMED FOR THE *DEFENCE*

Question by counsel - After the recess, did you see or hear any impolite language or conduct on the part of Vincent or Addison Witcher, or any of their friends, towards either of the Clements until the firing began

Answer - No

EXAMINATION IN CHIEF RESUMED

Question by counsel - Did you see, after the recess, any impolite conduct towards Capt. Witcher or any of his friends, by any of the Messrs. *Clements*

Answer - No

ROBERT MITCHELL

DEPOSITION OF JACOB G. MACKENHAMER

Jacob G. Mackenhamer being called and sworn, says:

That I was at Dickinson''s on Saturday last, at the taking of some depositions. In the afternoon they were about to resume the business of the day, as I stepped into the room. I heard Vincent Witcher suggesting the propriety of adjourning over until Monday, on the grounds that the examination of the witness could not be got through with that afternoon, and that she would consequently be in the hands of the opposite party. At that point, I think that Ralph Clement remarked that she could be placed under the care of the court or in jail, he *did'nt* care which. The court, Robert Mitchell, remarked that he should do nothing of the kind. Vincent Witcher still pressed his desire that it should be continued, on the grounds that the witness would not be under the care of the opposite party that the opposite {party} might not have the advantage of dictating to {the witness} as they might have if the examination was commenced and adjourned over unfinished. Ralph Clement remarked, that she was not under his keeping or under his care. Vincent Witcher replied that whoever said that told a damned lie. Ralph Clement rose to his feet when he made that remark, but immediately resumed his seat. Vincent Witcher said you had better make your remark more direct. Ralph Clement made some remark that I could not catch, but immediately there was a general stir in the room, and a firing of pistols. I did not see any one shoot. I do not know who fired first. I do not know who fired at all. My first effort was to get out of the room. I heard as many as four shots before I succeeded. That is all I can say that I saw or heard at that time. I remained out at the end of the house until the firing had ceased. Persons were coming out. Among others my attention was attracted to a young man particularly, who seemed to be in pain, holding one arm, with a knife or dirk in the other hand, it bloody. John Anthony Smith, was the man alluded to *some one* accompanied him to the house so far as I saw I could not say that I recognized *any one* else, particular under the excitement.

Question by the counsel for the prosecution. Did you return in the room after the firing ceased

Answer - I did in the course of two or three minutes

Question - What did you see

Answer - I found James Clement lying dead near the door in a considerable pool of blood with his knife grasped in his hand unsheathed a little further in the room near the center I saw William Clement lying dead he lay in somewhat a coiled position, with his arm crooked but rather extended, the fore-finger pointing straight with a pistol lying across his arm, about half way between the wrist and the elbow I made no examination of the pistol nor did I take it in my hand a little further still in the room I saw Ralph Clement lying on the floor, his head supported by a man by the name of Baker I believe apparently badly wounded Colo. Carter seemed to be affording him what relief he could by bathing his face, I believe, with camphor, or spirits and camphor. Colo. Carter, Mr. Baker and myself and Charles Powell, I believe, assisted to put him on the bed he appeared to suffer very much - something like an hour and a half from that time he died

Question - After Mr. Ralph Clement denied that the witness was under his charge, and said that she might be sent to jail if the magistrate wished it, did Capt. Witcher still persist in his motion for an adjournment of the taking of depositions

Answer - I should say that he did

Question - When Capt. Witcher first said that he was unwilling to the adjournment because the witness would be with Ralph Clement, did Mr. Clement retort upon Capt. Witcher in an angry manner

Answer - No, he did not

Question - When Ralph Clement had pronounced it a damned lie, how often had Capt. Witcher made a statement calling forth the damned lie

Answer - I should suppose that it was the second time - he having stated that he wanted the adjournment so as to have her removed from any dictation and, secondly, that he had understood that she was under his care

Question - At the time that Mr. Clement rose from his seat what was his manner and language

Answer - His manner was somewhat abrupt, and his language was, that whoever said so told a damned lie

Question - Did he immediately resume his seat

Answer - He did

Question - Was your attention directed to Mr. Clement at the time he arose from his seat

Answer - Particularly

Question - When he arose from his seat did you see any indications of an effort to draw any weapon

Answer - I did not

Question - What was Capt. Witcher"s position and what did he do

Answer - I was somewhat in rear of Ralph Clement at the time and inclined to his left there was an opening before me and Capt. Witcher so that I could distinctly see his face he was sitting on a chair as I think in an opposite direction to Ralph Clement Capt. Witcher seemed to meditate a moment and remarked that, he, Clement had better make his position or remark more direct

Question - In reply to the remarks of Capt. Witcher, of which you have just spoken, did Mr. R. Clement say anything at all

Answer - He said something, but I could not catch a word of what he said, as at that moment the whole house was aroused or I will say that there was a general stir in the house

Question - How long do you suppose it was after Capt. Witcher told Mr. Clement, "that he had better make his remark more direct", before the firing began

Answer - It was almost instantly

Question - From what part of the room did it appear or seem to you that the first fire came

Answer - I am unable to give any satisfactory answer

Question - After the firing was over, did you examine the pistol of Mr. Ralph Clement, and had it been discharged or not

Answer - I assisted in taking off the belt. I found his pistol in the pocket of his belt, and while drawing the belt from under the body, assisted by Colo. Carter, he took the pistol out of its pocket. I did not take hold of the pistol, nor do I know whether it was loaded or not. I saw no knife in the belt

Question - Did the firing, after it began, continue without intermission to the end, or was there a slight cessation and a resumption of the firing

Answer - The firing was more rapid at its commencement than it was at its close, but there was no cessation from the commencement

Question - Who was with Capt. Witcher when he came into the counting-room to resume the taking of depositions

Answer - I do not know particularly

Question - Was John Anthony Smith, Vincent O. Smith, Samuel Swanson, and Addison Witcher in the room at the time the taking of the depositions commenced, or about that time, or either of any of them

Answer - About the time they met to resume the taking of the depositions, I recollect seeing Addison Witcher and Samuel Swanson in the room the others I have no recollection of seeing

Question - When you saw Mr. Swanson did he have a stick in his hand

Answer - I saw him as I see any other man in a dense crowd I did not see the stick if he had one

Question - Did you see Mr. William and James Clement If so, what was their position

Answer - I did not see them to recognize them at that time

Question - Did you examine the floor near where Ralph Clement was lying, and *do* you find any bullet-holes near there

Answer - I did not examine the floor nor neither did I find any bullet-holes near where he was lying

Question - Did you see Mr. Ralph Clement between the time of his being wounded and his death. If so, state whether or not he retained his senses

Answer - I saw him between the time of his being wounded and his death, and he appeared to retain his senses, I should say up to within some fifteen minutes of the time of his dying and think he retained his senses as long as he did his speech

Question - How many shots do you suppose were fired

Answer - Between twenty and twenty-five I would suppose

CROSS EXAMINATION BY COUNSEL FOR *DEFENCE*

Question - When Vincent Witcher applied for the continuance of the disposition, to whom did he address himself

Answer - To the court, or to Robert Mitchell, sitting as the court

Question - Did he not continue to address himself to the magistrate when he was stating that the witness would be left in the hands of the other party

Answer - He continued to address himself to the magistrate until the collision of words between himself and Ralph Clement

Question - Who commenced that collision

Answer - Ralph Clement''s language was the offensive language first

Question - To whom did Ralph Clement address himself as shown either by his words, looks or gestures, when he there spoke the offensive words

Answer - My opinion was they were addressed to Vincent Witcher

Question - What length of time did you pay attention to the taking of the depositions in the case then before the magistrate

Answer - I was frequently in the room, and was there some hours in all during the time the depositions were being taken I was there on Thursday in the afternoon and frequently during the day of Friday and Saturday

Question - During that time, who was managing the case for the plaintiff and who for the defendant

Answer - Ralph Clement was managing for the defendant, and a gentleman by the name of Dabney a part of the time, during Thursday and part of Friday. What time of day Dabney left on Friday I do not recollect. The balance of the time, Addison Witcher for the plaintiff, to the best of my recollection, during the time I was present

Question - Was not Vincent Witcher all the time

Answer - Generally speaking he was, though I had seen him leave the room once or twice

Question - During the whole of that time in proceeding to take the depositions, did not the said Vincent and Addison Witcher invariably address themselves to the magistrate, and conduct themselves in the most courteous and polite manner towards the defendant and his parents, until the collision occurred between Vincent Witcher and Ralph A. Clement, which you have before stated

Answer - I cannot say invariably. There was one occasion upon which Vincent Witcher evinced some feeling in a remark to Ralph Clement, the words which were, "I am not addressing myself to you sir". They were drawn from Mr. Witcher by some remark from Mr. Clement, while Mr. Witcher was addressing the court, and spoken with some warmth by Mr. Witcher with that exception, Mr. Witcher"s course was mild and deliberate throughout up to the unfortunate collision. I cannot say invariably with regard to Addison Witcher. On one occasion he remarked "he did not care whether he, Ralph Clement, was satisfied, if the court was satisfied" with that exception, his manner was deliberate in conducting the examination

Question - What caused the remark from Addison Witcher

Answer - I am unable to say, but it was from something said by Mr. Clement, but I was unable to distinguish the words

Question - On the two occasions on which you have stated that warm words were used by Vincent and Addison Witcher, *did'nt* the matter pass off with *there* words

Answer - Yes

Question - When Ralph Clement arose from his seat stating that "Whoever said so told a damned lie", did Vincent Witcher get up

Answer - He did not, so far as I could see

Question - In an answer to a previous question put by the *commonwealth*, in which you stated that the magistrate, Mitchell, said that he would do nothing of the kind, did you understand him to mean continuing the deposition, or taking the witness into custody

Answer - I understood him to refuse taking the witness into custody and to continue the deposition at that time

Question - State the position of the parties who were interested in the matter, immediately before the first pistol was fired

Answer - Capt. Witcher was sitting by the bed on a chair, I suppose on nearly the opposite side of the table, but not directly opposite to Ralph Clement the magistrate sat between the window and the table Ralph Clement was sitting at the table on the left of the magistrate. I saw Miss Bennett the witness I think she was sitting down but her position I cannot point out

Question - Did Vincent Witcher do anything at the time he was meditating as you have stated

Answer - Nothing that I know of or saw

Question - Did Ralph Clement rise or attempt to do so at the time he made the reply to Vincent Witcher, which you say you did not hear

Answer - I do not know

Question - Did you examine the body of Ralph Clement after he was shot, or before, thoroughly, with a view to ascertain what arms he had

Answer - I did not

Question - Why do you judge that there were between twenty and twenty-five shots fired that day

Answer - By my believing that I heard that many reports, though I did not count

Question - Where were you standing when the first pistol was fired

Answer - I suppose I was moving to get out of the room under the impression that there would be firing

Question - From the time you last saw Vincent Witcher sitting in his chair by the bed, as you have stated, and when Ralph Clement said something which you say you did not understand or recollect, until the first shot, was it possible for Vincent Witcher to have changed his position, drawn a pistol and fired in that interval

Answer - I suppose I was moving to get out of the room under the impression that there would be firing

Question by same – From the time you last saw Vincent Witcher sitting in his chair by the bed, as you have stated, and when Ralph Clement said something which you say you did not understand or recollect until the first shot was it possible for Vincent Witcher to have changed his position drawn a pistol and fired in that interval

Answer – I should suppose that was possible

EXAMINATION IN CHIEF RESUMED

Question by counsel for prosecution - Were not the first abrupt words you heard used by Mr. Ralph A. Clement just before the firing, in reply to the remark Capt. Witcher had made about the witness being left in his charge

Answer - I believe they were

Question - Did you at any time see or hear Mr. William C. Clement, in any wise interfere with the taking of the depositions, or in any manner insult Capt. Witcher or any of his friends on that occasion

Answer - I did not

Question - Did you see Mr. William Clement"s body after he was shot. If so, state the most prominent wounds about him you saw

Answer - I saw him after he was shot. I saw him partially stripped. I saw various wounds upon him, the number I do not recollect the most prominent seemed to be a stab in the belly and a shot in the eye

Question - Was not the skin around the bullet-holes at the eye apparently burnt, and were not his eye-brows and eye lashes singed off

Answer - I am not able to say

Question - Was not his throat cut

Answer - I looked at the body, I saw there was a gash on the neck which I did not examine

Question - At what period of the taking of the depositions was it that Mr. Addison Witcher remarked that he did not care whether Mr. Ralph Clement was satisfied or not, so the court was

Answer - I am unable to say whether it was on the second or third day

Question - Did Mr. Ralph Clement reply harshly to that remark of Mr. A. Witcher"s

Answer - I cannot tell I heard him say something in an under tone

CROSS EXAMINATION RESUMED

Question by counsel for *defence* - Are not the abrupt word which you alluded to in your answer to the first question put by the *commonwealth* on your second examination by it the damned lie which you mentioned in a previous part of your deposition

Answer - They were

EXAMINATION RESUMED IN CHIEF

Question by counsel for prosecution - Was not the damned lie given by Mr. Ralph Clement to the authority upon which Capt. Witcher made his charge, about the witness being under his control or keeping, before she was introduced as a witness

Answer - It certainly was intended to be given to the authority, but addressed to Mr. Witcher according to my opinion

JACOB G. MACKENHAMER

Adjourned over till to-morrow morning 8 o''clock.
BENJAMIN F. COOPER, J.P.

Thursday morning March 1st 1860. Court met pursuant to adjournment same justice as on yesterday.

DEPOSITION OF GRESHAM CHOICE

Gresham Choice being called and sworn says:

I was in the counting-room at the time the affray occurred, consequently I know nothing of the circumstances under which James Clement came to his death. I was out of doors some twenty or twenty-five steps from the scene of action when the firing commenced as soon as I heard the firing I started to the room, got near the end of the porch met a number of gentlemen rushing out of the room about that time the firing was going on furiously. I advanced no farther toward the room until the firing ceased - I then went into the room. The first thing that attracted my attention was James R. Clement lying on the floor, with his head near the door leading from the store into the counting-room and appeared to be entirely dead. I could not well pass into the room without stepping over his head and shoulders. After looking at him a few seconds I stepped over him, and William Clement was lying on the floor and appeared also to be dead. At about that time Ralph A. Clement was also on the floor near the writing desk, and seemed to be struggling to get up which he did not succeed in doing, and declared himself a murdered man or a dying man, I am not certain which at that time but am certain he afterwards said several times that he was a dying man. A few minutes after Colo. Carter and some other gentlemen took him up and put him on the bed, where he lived, perhaps, two hours, or two-and-half, and died. I saw him die

Question by counsel for *commonwealth* - State what was the condition of Ralph A. Clement"s mind from the time he was shot to the time of his death

Answer - Judging from his conversation he appeared to be perfectly in his senses until, perhaps, within some thirty minutes of his death

Question - State whether you believe from what you saw of Ralph Clement at that time, that he was satisfied that he could not recover and would soon die

Answer - Certainly he declared several times that he was dying.

Question - State anything he may have said after he had become convinced that he had to die, relative to the whole matter, up to the time that you believe he lost his mind

Answer - Soon after he was laid on the bed, he seemed to become a little more composed he then called for the magistrate and said he wished to make a dying declaration - the magistrate was not in the room at that time, that I now recollect. Some minutes afterwards he said he wanted to see Robert Mitchell. Mr. Mitchell then went to his bed-side, and he went on to make a tolerable lengthy statement to Mr. Mitchell, the magistrate, and said it was his dying declaration Mr. Mitchell turned *roun* the bed and came to where I was, and I suggested to the magistrate that it would be best to reduce that declaration to writing that I thought it was his privilege to make such a declaration, and the law required it to be in writing thereupon Mr. Mitchell requested me to do the writing. I refused to do so told him I never had done such a thing. He then turned to Mr. Mackenheimer, asked Mr. Mackenheimer to do it Mr. Mackenheimer also refused to do it.

They came to me a second time to do it and I done it. The following is a copy of the paper referred to:

"The following is the declaration of Ralph A. Clement, as his dying declaration, relative to the shooting of himself and brothers, made before me, Robert Mitchell a justice of the peace for Franklin *county*, this 25th day of February, 1860, that is:

"I never attempted to draw an arm. Addison Witcher *catched* me and held me around the waist and arms and told them to come and shoot me – a damned rascal. I was shot several times while in that fix, and he held me until I fell – numbers of pistols were fired at me then"

Robert Mitchell   Witness: Gresham Choice

Ralph A. Clement requested me to tell father that he wanted him to make the deed to my wife and child, according to my will

ROBERT MITCHELL

Question - When you went in the room after the firing was over, how far was Mr. James Clement lying from the foot of the bed

Answer - His feet was very near the foot of the bed

Question - Did it seem from his position that he had fallen from the bed

Answer - I cannot tell, his feet was very near the bed, and his head in an opposite direction from the foot of the bed

Question - In what part of the room was the bed located

Answer - Entering from the door leading from the store into the counting-room, the bed was directly before you, and in the corner on the left of the fire-place going in at that door

Question - Was there any blood near James Clement If so, state the extent of it

Answer - There was a considerable quantity of blood running from his head down by his side towards the fire-place

Question - In what position did he lie

Answer - He was lying on his back, or nearly so, with his head turned to the right side his left arm was lying on the floor by his side, his right hand resting on the handle or hilt of a bowie- knife or dirk, I suppose a bowie-knife, clenched

Question - Suppose his body had been raised up perpendicularly, would his front or his back have been next to the bed
Answer - His body would have been fronting the bed, and his head turned to the right

Question - Where about on the floor was the body of William Clement"s lying and in what position

Answer - The body of William Clement was between the body of James Clement and the fireplace his head resting near the centre of the room, I think, and his feet towards the bed. He was lying on his back, or nearly so, and his head, I think turned a little to one side his feet pointed obliquely to the right hand corner {can"t read} of the foot of the bed as you enter the room from the store door

Question - Did you discover any wounds upon his person If so, state what their character *ware*}, and where they were

Answer - At that time I discovered but one wound, and that was near the right eye. I was a witness in the room before the coroner"s inquest after the body was stripped. I then saw a number of wounds on his body. He had one wound on the neck just under the jaw a lengthy rash it appeared to be inflicted by a bowie-knife. He was stabbed in several places, at one of which, his intestines had come out. I think on the right side just below his ribs. I can"t undertake to describe the gun shot or bullet wounds, but there was a number of them

Question - Was there much blood about or immediately around the body of Mr. William Clement

Answer - Not a great deal

Question - Did the skin around the wound near the eye, appear to be blackened or scorched by the fire of the pistol, and the brows and eye-lashes to be singed

Answer - The skin around the wound near the eye, was of a dark appearance as though it had been powder-burnt

Question - Did you see any of the parties leaving the room after {the} encounter If so, state who they were, and whether or not they had weapons or blood about them

Answer - I saw a number of gentlemen leave the room about the time I entered it, or very soon afterwards. I do not recollect them all. I saw Capt. Witcher, and his son, Addison Witcher, and Mr. Samuel Swanson. I saw no weapons, nor neither did I see any blood upon either of the last named gentlemen. I saw several others that I did not recognize

Question - Did you see a stick in Mr. Samuel Swanson"s hands

Answer - Not that I recollect of

Question - Did you perceive any intermission in the firing after it began

Answer - There was, I think, an intermission of a second and a-half or two seconds after the first fire, and then the firing was very rapid, except a few of the last shots which appeared to be more deliberate or slower

Question - Were you in the room before dinner, when the proposition was made to postpone the further taking of depositions for that day

Answer - I was not

CROSS EXAMINE

Question by the counsel for the *defence* - You have stated that after the first fire there was a slight intermission do you not mean that you heard one single fire, and then the intermission issued

Answer - I do after the first fire there was a slight intermission, then the second fire, and from that time it was very rapid until near its close, when a few of the last shots became slower

Question - State whether you were present during the taking of the depositions there before the magistrate. If you were, how long were you present

Answer - I was present on last Saturday, probably about two hours while they were taking one deposition before dinner I was there after dinner but saw no depositions taken I do not recollect that I was in the room until after the affray

Question - Who was attending to the deposition for the parties on both sides of the suit

Answer - Mr. Ralph Clement seemed to conduct the taking on the one side, and Mr. Addison Witcher on the other Capt. Witcher and others were there

Question - State who are the parties to this suit

Answer - I know not

Question - Was not the conduct of Addison and Vincent Witcher during the time you were present, perfectly courteous and polite

Answer - As far as I saw, it was

EXAMINATION IN CHIEF RESUMES

Question by counsel for the *commonwealth* - What was the conduct of William Clement to Capt. Witcher and Addison Witcher as far as you saw

Answer - Entirely courteous and gentlemanly he did not seem to meddle with it in any way. I thought the whole parties were getting along remarkably well

GRESHAM CHOICE

DEPOSITION OF JAMES KEMP

James Kemp being called and sworn, says:

Question by the counsel for the *commonwealth*. Were you at Dickinson''s store on Saturday last, between the hours of 10 A.M. and 2 o''clock, P.M

Answer - I was

Question - State whether you know anything of a difficulty that took place, at that place, at that time, if so, state all you know about it

Answer - I do not know anything about it

Question - State if you were in the counting-room of Dickinson''s store on that day. If so, state whether there were any depositions taken there that day

Answer - I was there that day. I heard Mrs. Shelton''s evidence given in, but she was giving her evidence when I got there

Question - Do you know of the deposition of any person also being proposed to be taken there at that time

Answer - There was a lady brought forward that said she was going to give her evidence. I have seen the lady passing frequently I did not see her face during the time, but think they said her name was Betsy Bennett

Question - State anything that occurred at the time it was proposed to take her deposition

Answer - I think Vincent Witcher *named* that they had better put it off till Monday, because he lived a good ways from here and he wanted to go home. I think Mr. Witcher said he wanted his dinner I think they all rose up pretty much and came up here to dinner, and the *Clement's* had something with them to eat, and went out late into the road and *eat* it. After Mr. Witcher came back from dinner I think that there was something said again about Mr. Witcher wanting to go home that he lived at a distance and to go into the testimony of that lady he knew they couldn''t get through that night and to leave her in the hands of the opposite party he didn''t think it would be a fair trial or fair shake, or something like that. Ralph Clement said she wouldn''t be left in his hands, and said any person said so said a lie. Capt. Witcher rose up from his chair and made a little advance towards Mr. Clement and said some word I didn''t understand there was a fire made pretty quick who made it I didn''t know, I heard it but didn''t see it

Question - When Capt. Witcher rose and advanced towards Ralph Clement, did he attempt to draw a weapon

Answer - If he did, I didn''t see it

103

Question - Did you see Capt. Witcher put his hand in his bosom, when he rose and advanced towards Ralph Clement

Answer - I did not

Question - Do you know in what part of the room the first pistol was discharged

Answer - I do not

Question - How long did you remain in the room, after the discharge of the first pistol

Answer - I can't tell you, but no longer than I could get out

Question - Did not you start to leave the room as soon as Capt. Witcher rose and advanced towards Ralph Clement

Answer - I did

Question - What induced you to leave at that time

Answer - Because I had heard that both parties was pretty ambitious, and thought I had better get out

CROSS EXAMINATION

Question by counsel for the *defence* - In the remarks about the continuance, to whom did Vincent Witcher address himself

Answer - I thought it was to the justice, Mitchell

Question - Did he not call him the court

Answer - I think he did

Question - When he said the witness would be in the hands of the opposite party, was he not still addressing himself to the magistrate

Answer - I think he was

Question - When the lie was given, did the magistrate call to order, or offer to protect Vincent Witcher from mistreatment

Answer - I never heard it

Question - Where were you standing at this time

Answer - I was sitting on the side of the bed near the foot, my face towards the table where they were taking depositions

Question - Where was Ralph Clement *setting* when he gave the lie and did he not rise from his seat as he gave the lie

Answer - I think Ralph Clement was standing up with some papers in his hands *sorter* folding them up. He was standing at the table, I think

Question - What reply did Ralph Clement make to the words which Vincent Witcher spoke, and which you did not hear distinctly

Answer - I never heard Ralph Clement speak a word

Question - Did you hear the word "picking the witness", made use of

Answer - Mr. Witcher named something of that sort, but I can't remember what it was

Question - Who was on the bed with you

Answer - I don't know

EXAMINATION IN CHIEF RESUMED

Question by counsel for *commonwealth* - Did you see Mr. James Clement, at or about the time you were on the bed

Answer - I did not

Question. Did you see William Clement at that time

Answer. I did not

JAMES KEMP

DEPOSITION OF JOHN C. HUTCHERSON

John C. Hutcherson being called and sworn says:

I suppose that I got into the counting-room of Dickinson''s store on Saturday last about one o''clock. When I stepped into the door I saw Ralph Clement sitting by the side of a little table seemed to be in the act of writing or looking over papers I went around and took a stand near the fire-place with my back to the fire. The first thing I knew of Capt. Witcher he was sitting at my right side against the bed, and said something about the deposition of a certain lady sitting before the fire. I thought Capt. Witcher was disposed to have the deposition taking adjourned over until Monday. Mr. Ralph A. Clement seemed desirous it should go on. Capt. Witcher was making some remarks to the justice his remarks was, I think, he was opposed to going into it, without there was time to complete it and he didn''t think there was and I think, said something about the witness would be in the hands of the opposite party. Clement remarked that she could be placed under guard, or anywhere satisfactory that he shouldn''t be with her. Capt. Witcher''s reply was, that she had been under their control for some time. Clement said that any man said she had been under his control was a liar. Capt. Witcher paused, I thought, a very short time asked him to make that more direct or personal or if he did make that direct, or personal, or something to that effect. Capt. Witcher then commenced rising up in a position which caused me to believe that he was fixing to get arms, raising his hands. I then aimed to walk out and look back and see what they done before I stopped to look back a pistol was fired. I pursued on, and immediately another pistol was fired. I was passing on and as I got near the door I rather turned my head and saw the flash of a pistol - the ball passed through a lock of my hair and then I left. After the shooting was over, I went into the house by the end door of the porch I stepped over James Clement lying before the door dead. William Clement was lying near the middle of the floor dead. Ralph A. Clement lying near, or rather against the writing desk he seemed to be very much wounded and said he was bound to die

Question by counsel for *commonwealth* - You say that Capt. Witcher raised his hands in such a way as to lead you to believe that he intended drawing arms. How did he place his hands as to produce this impression upon your mind

Answer - I do not know

Question - Who fired the first pistol on that occasion

Answer - I do not know

Question - Did you see any person fire a pistol on that occasion if so, who was it

Answer - I did. Capt. Witcher fired the third pistol, I think

Question - Where was Capt. Witcher standing at the time of the first fire

Answer - At the head of the bed, near the fire-place

Question - From what direction was the first pistol fired

Answer - It was on the same side of the house, near the bed

Question - Did you see James Clement at the time you started to leave the room if so, where was he

Answer - I did not

Question - Did you see William Clement if so, where was he

Answer - I did not

Question - State as near as you can, the words used by Capt. Witcher upon the subject of the continuance of the deposition, and the witness being left in the care of the opposite party

Answer - He seemed to be holding some little argument with squire Mitchell he seemed that he didn't wish to go into trial without they could complete it that the witness would be left in the hands of the opposite party. Clement remarked that she should be placed under guard then Capt. Witcher remarked that they had had her under their control for some time. Clement said any man said he had her under his control was a liar

Question - When Capt. Witcher arose up from his seat, was his manner and expression of countenance angry or otherwise

Answer - I don't know

Question - How far had you gone, after starting, before you heard the first pistol fire

Answer - i suppose, probably, eight or ten feet

CROSS EXAMINED

Question by counsel for the *defence* - What was the position of Ralph Clement when he gave the lie

Answer - Sitting at the table

Question - Did he rise when he gave it

Answer - I think not

Question - Did he rise after he gave it

Answer - A short time after he gave it he arose

107

Question - At what time did he rise

Answer - When Capt. Witcher asked for that explanation. When I turned my head from Capt. Witcher, I looked towards Clement, and he was rising

Question - What did Ralph Clement say

Answer - If he said anything, I never heard him

Question - Had Vincent Witcher straightened himself up entirely

Answer - I think he had about got *strait* before Clement rose

Question - Did Ralph Clement do anything while rising

Answer - When I saw him rising, I turned off and never saw him *any more*

Question - What was the position of his hands, when you last saw him rising

Answer - I do not know

Question - How far had he risen when you last saw him in the act of rising

Answer - I do not think he was *strait* up

Question - Was his middle above the table

Answer - I cannot say it was or not

Question - While Vincent Witcher was pausing, did he not sit still in his chair

Answer - He did

Question - Who was on the bed

Answer - I do not know

Question - Was any person on the bed

Answer - I think there was

Question - How many

Answer - I can't say

Question - At the time of your leaving your position near the bed, were there not several persons *wither lying* or sitting the bed

Answer - I do not know

Question - If Ralph Clement mad no reply to Vincent Witcher, do you know any cause that induced Vincent Witcher to rise and draw a weapon

Answer - I don't know of any cause but the remark he made.

Question - At the time of the first fire was not your back turned to Vincent Witcher

Answer - It was

Question - In the reply that Vincent Witcher made to the lie, when given by Ralph Clement do you recollect Witcher's exact words

Answer - I do not

Question - When Vincent Witcher made his remarks, about the witness being left in the hands of the opposite party, was he not addressing himself to the magistrate

Answer - I think he was

Question - Did you not state to John A. Smith, in this house, on the day before yesterday, in the presence of Samuel D. Berger, that when Ralph A. Clement gave the lie to Vincent Witcher you expected Vincent Witcher to attack him but to your surprise, the fire came from the other side, or words to the above amount

Answer - I did, after this ball passed me. I took it for granted that there must have been somebody on the side of the house where I had not expected there was any enemy, from not seeing any person on that side of the room in a position of making any motion towards shooting. By Capt. Witcher shooting to that door, I took it for granted that there must have been somebody on that side, as the shooting had all been in that direction

Adjourned until to-morrow morning, 9 o'clock.
                BENJAMIN F. COOPER, J.P.

Friday morning, March 2d, 1860.

Court met pursuant to adjournment same justice as on yesterday. John C. Hutchenson, being recalled, the cross examination was continued

Question by counsel for the *defence* - From what part of the room did the report of the first pistol proceed

Answer - It was on my right as I walked from the fire-place to the store-room door

Question - Had Vincent Witcher advanced any toward Ralph Clement before you turned to go to the store-door

Answer - He had not

Question - Was there any interval to be observed between the first shot and the others

Answer - There was a very short period between them all

Question - Was there not a longer interval between the first and second fire than between the second and any that followed it

Answer - I cannot say whether there was or not, they all being fired very quick

Question - How near was Vincent Witcher to the head of the bed when you turned off

Answer - He was standing against his chair, which was *setting* against the bed

Question - Just before turning off, were you standing between a line that might have been drawn from Vincent to the store-room and the bed

Answer - I was not

Question - What part of the room do you allude to in a previous answer, when you said that the fire came from a part of the room in which you supposed there was no enemy

Answer - It came from the right of the room as I walked from the fire-place to the back part of the counting-room to go out at the door

Question - To whom did you refer, in the answer just referred to, when you said you supposed there was no enemy

Answer - Before the third pistol fire, I supposed it to be Capt. Witcher leaving him on that side of the room, and seeing nobody else making any movements in any way but, after the third fire coming in the direction it did, I thought there must have been an *attact* made on him by somebody that I did not see

Question - At the time you moved from the fire-place, how many, and what persons were near Ralph Clement on his side of the table

Answer - If there were any persons near him I did not notice them

EXAMINATION IN CHIEF RESUMED

Question by counsel for *commonwealth* - Was Capt. Witcher on your right while you *was* standing at the fire-place

Answer - He was

Question - How far from the hearth was the chair, out of which you have stated Capt. Witcher arose

Answer - It was very near the hearth

Question - Was it on it

Answer - I can"t say exactly it was against the bed

Question - In going from where you were standing to the door of the store in a *strait* line, would not Capt. Witcher have been upon the right

Answer - I think he would, in the way I walked out from the fire

Question - Did you see the flash of the third pistol, the ball of which passed so near you

Answer - I did

Question - In whose hands was it

Answer - I think it was Capt. Witcher

Question - Had you heard any firing before you saw that flash that did seem to come immediately from Capt. Witcher, or very near him

Answer - It was from the same side of the room but whether it was as far back as he stood I can"t say

Question - Can you state, with any satisfactory certainty to yourself, the exact place from which any of the fire came - except the flash you saw

Answer - I cannot. I do not expect if I had not turned to go out at the door that I should have seen that

Question - Have you seen a chair struck by a ball near the top and ranging obliquely across the chair, near the side of the front room of the chair

Answer - I have not

Question - Was Mr. Ralph A. Clement *setting* in a chair at the last sight you had of him before the firing began

Answer - I think not

Question - Where was he, and what was his position, the last time you saw him before the firing

Answer - He was rising up

Question - Did you observe the position of the chair to the table in which he had been *setting*

Answer - I did not

Question - When the angry words begun between Capt. Witcher and Mr. R. Clement, did you have to turn around before you made a start for the store-door

Answer - I did not. I was standing fronting of the store-room

Question - From the number of rounds upon the dead, and the number of bullet-holes about the room, and the time the firing lasted, must not more than one pistol have fired at the same time

Answer - I cannot say for they were firing a considerable time

Question - While you was standing near the fire-place, or at any time thereabouts, did you see Mr. Addison Witcher

Answer - I don't remember seeing him at all that day

Question - What induced you to make the communication to Mr. John A. Smith, about which you have been interrogated or questioned

Answer - It was from the fact of talking about the ball that passed me

Question - Who started the conversation

Answer - I think he commenced laughing at me about the ball as he was *lieing* on the bed

Question - Having stated that you did not know any cause for Capt. Witcher firing at Mr. Clement, state whether or not you did not know of an angry family *law suit* and *feiud* between the parties and their immediate relations

Answer - I had understood there was such a suit as that going on, and supposed that they were taking that deposition for that purpose as for knowing the fact, I did not

Question - Did you start to leave the room because of the danger you thought you were in, from a possible firing between Capt. Witcher and Mr. Ralph *Clement's*

Answer - I did, or using bowie-knives, or something of that sort

CROSS EXAMINATION RESUMED

Question by counsel for the *defence* - When you was standing near the hearth with your face towards *to* store-door, was not Vincent Witcher"s position considerably nearer to the end of the room, next to the head of the bed, than yours was

Answer - I was standing very near where he was sitting as near his feet, pretty, as I could. I was standing on the same side of the fire-place where he was sitting

Question - Was your face, side or back, opposite to Vincent Witcher"s face

Answer - My side was opposite to his face had to turn up head to look at him

EXAMINATION IN CHIEF RESUMED

Question by counsel for *commonwealth* - Was the back of Capt. Witcher"s chair to the side of the bed

Answer - I do not know I think likely though that it was.

JOHN C. HUTCHERSON.

Note to John C. Hutcherson"s deposition. He wishes to state that he made a mistake in saying that after the firing he entered the counting-room by the end door of the porch, that instead of that door he entered the counting-room by the door leading from the store into the counting- room.
JOHN C. HUTCHERSON
{This note appears after the deposition of James M. Hutcherson on the original record.}

DEPOSITION OF JAMES M. HUTCHERSON

James M. Hutcherson, being called and sworn, says:

Question by counsel for *commonwealth* - State anything you may know of this affair between Messrs Clements and the prisoners

Answer - I heard Mr. Vincent Witcher say something about having a deposition laid over until another day, as the{y} couldn''t get through that day with the lady. Mr. Ralph Clement said that he had no objections, provided they put a *gueard* over her, or put her in some one''s keeping, who would see that the other party did not converse with her, or something to that effect. Mr. Vincent Witcher said that he did not think this court or magistrate, or something of that sort, had any right to do that. Mr. Mitchell, the magistrate, said if he had a right to do it, he did not wish to exercise it. If Mr. Vincent Witcher said anything then, I did not hear him. Mr. Ralph Clement said that if anybody said that he had any *controal*, or something to that effect, over that room, told a lie. I turned around then and walked out of the room just as I got out of the room a pistol fired. When I returned to the room after the firing ceased, Mr. James Clement was lying near the door dead. Mr. William Clement''s I suppose it was him was *lieing* a little farther in the room dead Ralph Clement was on the bed

Question - When you were in the room last before the firing did you see Mr. Addison Witcher

Answer - I did not then. I had seen him in there in the morning before they took the recess

Question - Was Mr. Addison Witcher''s position generally, when you saw him, near Mr. Ralph Clement *setting* near together

Answer - I don''t know that it was

Question - Did you see James and William Clement in the room when you left

Answer - I did not

Question - After the firing had ceased, did you see any person with a knife, pistol, or stick, at or near the counting room

Answer - I saw Mr. John Smith run out of the counting-room with a knife in his hand, and I think he had a pistol in his hand too, I am not certain as to the pistol

Question - Was there any blood about him or his weapons

Answer - There was blood on his knife. I am not certain about any being on him

CROSS EXAMINATION

Question by counsel for *defence* - Are you certain that Ralph Clement said lie, or damned lie, or God damned lie

Answer - I understood to say lie

Question - Did he rise when gave the lie

Answer - I don"t think he did

Question - Where were you standing in the room

Answer - Standing near the door

Question - Did you look to see whether James and William Clement were in the room or not

Answer - I did not

JAS. M. HUTCHERSON.

DEPOSITION OF COLO. MADISON CARTER

Colo. Madison Carter being called and sworn, says:

That I was not in the room when the first pistol was fired. I had been in there a moment or two previous. When they were about to proceed to take the deposition of Miss Bennett. Capt. Vincent Witcher renewed his motion for an adjournment of taking the deposition of Miss Bennett addressing himself to the court, remarked substantially, as well as I recollect. If justice could be obtained or was likely to be obtained by commencing the taking of that deposition, when it could not be completed on that evening and leaving the witness in the care and control of the opposite party, to be conversed with as well as I recollect, until the next week or Monday. To which Mr. Ralph A. Clement replied, that the witness was not under his care or *controul*, and remarked that the court might take charge of the witness himself, put her at any other place or send her to jail if the law would allow him. Capt. Witcher then said, as well as I recollect, that he had understood or ben informed that Ralph A. Clement had brought her, the witness, there that day under his care and *controul* to which Ralph A. Clement replied, "if any person says I brought her here under my care or *controul* it is a lie.". I then shook my head at Ralph A. Clement, turned and started out of the room. Before I got out of the room I heard Capt. Witcher say, "make your supposition or charge", as well as I recollect, "more definite or explicit if you like." About the time I got to the door leading from the counting-room into the store, or perhaps one step inside of the store-room, a rush of persons came against me and threw me off to the left of the entrance way at that time the firing commenced in the room. As soon as I heard the firing commence I wheeled about and endeavored to make my entrance back into the room, but as often as I attempted it I was thrown back by persons rushing out, until the firing had nearly ceased. When I entered the room I saw James R. Clement lying dead on the floor, and some gentleman"s arm with a pistol in his hand, not more than two feet and-a-half, I think, from the body of James R. Clement, fire the pistol at him. I saw not the slightest movement in the body. I then passed over him, and a little farther in the room I saw William C. Clement *lieing* dead. I heard Ralph A. Clement complaining at the farther side of the room partly under the writing desk and partly not. I went to him, took him up and set him on the floor, and asked two or three gentlemen to assist me in laying him on the bed they did so. I remained with him, except a few moments, until he died. While I was endeavoring to enter the door from the store-room while the firing was going on, there was a vacancy occasioned by persons passing out that I saw into the room, at which moment I saw James R. Clement standing on the bed near the *centre* thereof, about three feet and towards us in a slightly curved position forward. I saw him no more the aperture closed until I saw him *lieing* dead at the foot of the bed

Question by counsel for the *commonwealth* - After the firing had ceased and you returned to the room, did you examine the wounds and the condition of the bodies If so, state how many rounds there were upon each body, and what the character of those rounds were

Answer - At that time, I did not, except so far as Ralph A. Clement was concerned. I endeavored, as well as I could, ascertain the number and locality of his wounds, to see whether they were mortal or not. I found on him six if not seven wounds two of which, were in his right shoulder a little back of the front part of his arm one across the left side of his head above the ear one on the right side of the spine, passing, as I judged, through the right kidney one through his left *fore* finger, and a glance on the left arm between the shoulder and elbow, as well as I recollect. After the death of Ralph A. Clement, I examined the body of William Clement very partially. I saw a hole shot in the bone of his right eye, which I considered mortal. I did not strip him at that time. After the body was stripped by the coroner, I saw upon his body various mortal wounds the number I do not know., not having counted them. He had a stab with a bowie-knife or dirk in his whiskers, striking about where the teeth entered the jaw-bone on the right jaw immediately under the jaw-bone there was a long and apparently deep gash on his right side below the ribs there was a gash through which a portion of his bowels had *protuded.* He had two other stabs that I recollect one on his right breast another just under the collar-bone, apparently inflicted with an elevated hand some three or four bullet-holes, or perhaps more. I did not count them around and about the *centre* of his chest. He had also a considerable cut on the muscle of the left arm. As to James R. Clement, I did not examine his wounds with as much particularity as I did the others, from the fact that he had some wounds in the breast that I believed had penetrated his heart, from the profusion of blood that had escaped. I saw upon his head near the top rather on the right side, where he had received two blows apparently from a stick. I saw across the right side of his forehead above the eye another bruise. I saw on his left arm several bruises that I judged were caused by a stick

Question - Did you examine the weapons of the deceased If so, state whether or not the pistols seemed to have been discharged, or their knives to have been drawn

Answer - I examined their weapons. I found the pistol of James R. Clement entirely discharged - every barrel – it was a five-shooter. His bowie-knife had not been drawn from the scabbard. William C. Clement"s pistol, a five-shooter, also, two barrels had been discharged his bowie- knife had not been drawn from the scabbard. Ralph A. Clement"s pistol, a five-shooter, also had not been taken from his belt nor fired his dirk, a small hand dirk, had not been taken from his pocket, nor had the newspaper scabbard, tied with a string, been removed

Question - Did the ball that you speak of going through the kidneys of Mr. Ralph Clement, strike him at right angles with the back

Answer - It seemed to have gone straight in. I did not probe it

Question - Did the skin around the wound on the eye of William Clement seem to be blackened or burnt with powder

Answer - Yes, it did

Question - How far do you suppose it is probably that the fire from an ordinary five-shooter would burn the skin

Answer - I can"t probably tell. I suppose from the size of the stain around the wound that the muzzle of the pistol must have been within a few inches the circumference of the stain not being larger than a quarter of a dollar

Question - How far was the cut under the jaw of Mr. William Clement from the carotid artery

117

Answer - It was immediately over and across the carotid artery whether it reached to it or went through it I cannot say. I opened the wound and saw it was very deep, but did not farther examine it

Question - Would not the cutting of that artery in a living person cause an immense profusion of blood

Answer - It certainly would

Question - Was there much blood where the body of Mr. William Clement was *lieing*

Answer - There was not

Question - Did you see any bullet-holes in the floor where Mr. Ralph Clement was *lieing*

Answer - I recollect to have seen one rather obliquely in the floor, near where I picked up the body of Ralph A. Clement. From the impression made in the floor it seemed to be a large one

Question - Have you examined a certain chair in the room If so, do you find upon it the traces of a ball

Answer - I have examined a chair and find upon it the traces of a ball, it seemed to have struck the slat next to the top one, near the right post it seems to have touched that and gone obliquely through the bottom and struck the inside of the opposite front post

Question - State whether Mr. Ralph A. Clement was sitting down the last time you saw him before you left the room

Answer - Yes, he was sitting down when I shook my head at him and turned to walk out of the room

Question - Do you know Capt. Witcher's position when you left the room

Answer - When I turned to leave the room Capt. Vincent Witcher was sitting in a chair by the side of the bed, near the hearth on the left hand side of the room

Question - If Capt. Witcher had risen and advanced a step or two towards Clement, would not the range of the ball upon the chair, if the said of the chair was turned toward him, have corresponded with the probable direction of a ball, if such had been fired from that position

Answer - It seems to me that the side of the chair would have to have been placed rather obliquely from Capt. Witcher, before the ball would have ranged directly from him to where I last saw Ralph A. Clement *setting*

Question - If the chair was in the oblique position to Capt. Witcher, would the range of the ball upon it, fired from the angle of Capt. Witcher"s position, after he had risen and advanced a step or so towards Clement, have corresponded with the range of the ball upon this chair

Answer - From the height of Capt. Witcher I believe it would

Question - Have you examined the south-west side of the room in which the combat took place If so, state if you find any balls fired into it

Answer - I have not examined it, so as to speak with sufficient certainty about it

Question - Do you know anything of the position of a bale of cotton in the room

Answer - I have not examined it, so as to speak with sufficient certainty about it

Question - Do you know anything of the position of a bale of cotton in the room

Answer - I do. I think it is nearly directly opposite to the fire-place at the west end of the room and near the *centre*

Question - You spoke heretofore of Capt. Witcher"s renewing his motion for the adjournment of the taking of the depositions. When had he made the motion before for the adjournment

Answer - He had made a motion to adjourn the farther taking of depositions at that time, just a few minutes before the recess

Question - When he renewed the motion for an adjournment, had it been before overruled by the justice

Answer - It has been overruled by the justice or court, as they called him, previous to the intermission

Question - At the time Capt. Witcher renewed his motion for the adjournment, where was Mr. Addison Witcher, Mrs. Samuel Swanson the two Mr. Smith"s

Answer - Mr. Addison Witcher, as well as I recollect, was on the south-side of the room set *fair* from the stair-steps. Mr. Swanson and the two young Mr. Smith"s I have no recollection where they were

Question - You state upon that motion Capt. Witcher remarked that he understood that the witness, Elizabeth Bennett, had been brought there that day under the care of Mr. Ralph Clement. Do you know how she got there, and who brought her

Answer - My recollection is that she came to Ralph Clement"s on that morning after breakfast, and come up here with William C. Clement, Ralph A. Clement, Mr. Shelton and myself

Question - From Ralph A. Clement''s conduct at the time you left the room, did you anticipate any difficulty between Ralph A. Clement and Capt. Witcher, or from any other occurrence at that time

Answer - I did not. If I had, I should have *staid* there and tried to have kept peace

Question - Did the rush of persons you speak of, overtake you before the firing began

Answer - About that time, as well as I recollect

Question - Was there any perceptible cessation of the firing from the   commencement to the end

Answer - I did not perceive any until near the close, when there was a slight commotion, and then a few more fires. I cannot say how many

Question - When you saw James *Clement's* down and fired at in that position, state where you were

Answer - I was entering the door from the store-room into the counting-room

Question - Who of the prisoners at that time did you recognize in the room

Answer - I do not know that I saw any of them my attention being called to the dead bodies and Ralph

Question - How long had the firing been going on when you saw Mr. James Clement standing on the bed

Answer - I can''t possibly say as to time, but I think the firing had reached about the half-way point

Question - Do you know where Mr. William and James Clement were, when you left the room just before the firing began

Answer - James R. Clement was *lieing* on the bed from head to foot not far from the front side thereof. William C. Clement had been *lieing* behind James R. Clement a short time previous thereto

Question - From Mr. James R. Clement''s position on the bed, if he had extended his arm in the position of firing, would he not have brought the muzzle of his pistol necessarily within a very few inches of the person of Capt. Witcher

Answer - If Capt. Witcher had remained where I last saw him, I think James R. Clement could have placed the muzzle of his pistol in direct contact with the person of Capt. Witcher

Question - Was Mr. James R. Clement a good pistol shot

Answer - I saw him make a few shots last fall, and he seemed to shoot clean

Question - How far was Mr. Ralph Clement sitting from the position occupied by Mr. Addison Witcher, when you saw him sitting by the stair-steps

Answer - Not more than about three feet according to the best of my judgment and recollection

CROSS EXAMINATION

Question by counsel for *defence* - State your position exactly when the lie was given by Ralph Clements

Answer - I was near the *centre* of the room, about equal distance from Ralph Clement and Capt. Witcher one on my left and the other on my right

Question - After the lie was given did not Vincent Witcher pause and seem to reflect awhile

Answer - My recollection is that he paused

Question - Why did you leave the room

Answer - I cannot possibly tell I know of no cause that induced me to leave

Question - Why did you shake your head to Ralph Clement

Answer - For the reason that I desired him to say nothing more that would be insulting

Question - Did he observe the shake of your head

Answer - He did, and I thought I observed a slight change in his countenance – he rather dropped his head. His countenance and manner induced me to believe that he would say no more

Question - Did the reply of Vincent Witcher induce you to pause or to apprehend that any difficulty would arise between the parties

Answer - It did not

Question - Why did you wish to get back

Answer - To see what was going on and to take part in the affray, if I deemed it proper

Question - Were you armed

Answer - I had one of Allen"s six barrel revolvers

Question - How long had you attended the taking of the depositions, and were you thus armed all the time

Answer - I attended from the commencement to the end, and was thus armed every day

Question - Were your arms so carried as to be discoverable to any person who might look with a view of informing himself of that fact

Answer - I cannot really say. I carried it in the breast-pocket of my dress-coat on the left, the *but-end* of the pistol sticking out, the pocket not being deep enough to conceal it

Question - At the time of this difficulty, did you have on an overcoat

Answer - I don''t think I had

Question – Was your coat buttoned?

Answer - No

Question - Had you been without your overcoat generally during the day

Answer - I can''t recollect whether I had or had not

Question - Do you remember whether you were without it during all or any part of any previous day of taking said depositions

Answer - I know I had it on sometimes, and I think I had it off sometimes, I think I used my shawl sometimes instead of my overcoat

Question - Could an observer desirous to know whether you were armed or not, be much better able to ascertain that fact when you had on the dress coat alone if the revolver was in it

Answer - I have no doubt that he could be much better able to observe it

Question - When you saw James Clement fired on near to the door did you know that he was dead except from the effect of the fire

Answer - I did not positively know it

Question - Did you callout to the man who was about to fire that he was dead

Answer - I did not

Question - Did not the smoke and the declension of the sun make the corner very dark where James Clement''s body lay, at the time it was fired at

Answer - Yes that portion of the room was considerably darkened

Question - Did you know what *armour* the three Clements had before they reached the store, whether on that day or during any other day of taking of the depositions

Answer - Ralph A. Clement had a five shooter and a small hand dirk William C. Clement had a five shooter and a bowie-knife James R. Clement had the same they had no other arms except their pocket-knives that I know of on that and each previous day

Question - When you examined the belt of Ralph Clement was his revolver undisturbed in the belt

Answer - I think it was to the best of my recollection

Question - Did you make any examination of the belt and revolver for the purpose of seeing whether the revolver had partly been drawn from the belt

Answer - I did not

Question - Had *any body* that you know of touched or got to Ralph Clement after the firing ceased, before you got to him

Answer - No person that I saw or know of

Question - On the day of the shooting did you see James Clement take off his overcoat and hang it up in the counting-room

Answer - I do not recollect that I dd. I saw him pull it off once and hang it up or lay it *way* but whether it was that day or some other day I can"t say, but I think he pulled it off every day

Question - Are you certain that you were the first person that approached Ralph Clement after the firing ceased

Answer - I am not there were other persons in the room when I got in

Question - Who were they

Answer - I can"t designate any particular person

Question - Were any of them near to or attending upon Ralph Clement

Answer - No, they were not that I know of

Question - State all the things that were *lieing* about his body on the floor

Answer - I don''t recollect seeing anything but some old papers and rubbish of some sort or another *lieing* under the desk

Question - State the condition of his clothing, particularly about the breast and waist

Answer - I think his vest was buttoned he complained of being too tightly bound I loosened his clothes even to his drawers I unbuckled his belt and Mr. Mackenheimer pulled it from under him, I believe

Question - How long was this after you got into the room

Answer - I can''t say, but I suppose not more than ten or fifteen minutes

Question - Might not persons have come to Ralph Clement and remained with him several minutes before your attention was directed to him

Answer - I presume they might before I went in there

Question - After your got in did you not spend *sometime* in viewing the remains of William and James Clement before you went on to Ralph

Answer - No, I went to Ralph very soon after I got in the room, merely stopping long enough at the body of James and William to satisfy myself that they were dead

Question - Who were the first that approached Ralph after you got to him

Answer - I think it was an old gentleman, an Englishman, by the name of Baker, came in first and then Mr. Mackenheimer and old Charles Powell. I asked them to assist me on the bed with him if they pleased

Question - Did either of them touch im until the proceeded to put him on the bed

Answer - I think not I had him sitting on the floor and holding him up

Question - Were you standing to his front or his back

Answer - I think I was standing to his left side with my right arm around his shoulders
Question - How many times a minute can a good shooter discharge a revolver

Answer - I have no idea never having shot one a dozen times in my life I *recon}* I never owned or carried one until recently, except one some seven or eight months ago I borrowed one and carried it one day

Question - Was not the cause of this recent *carring* of that weapon on apprehension that some, or all the parties to this affair might become involved with each other

124

Answer - It was

Question - Did you ever have any difficulty with any of these defendants

Answer - Never I had nothing against any of them

Question - Where did you live when this difficulty occurred

Answer - I lived on Big Dan River in the *county* of Patrick

Question - Did you not marry a sister of the deceased

Answer - She is said to be and I have no doubt is their sister

Question - When James Clement was *lieing* on the bed as you have stated, was he not touching or very nearly so, the chair on which Vincent Witcher was sitting

Answer - I don't think he was touching the chair from my recollection I don't think he was *lieing* more than a foot, if that, from the back of the chair

Question - Can you state why you so particularly remember so exactly the relative position of these parties

Answer - I have no reason for remembering their relative positions except the mere fact of seeing them

Question - You have stated that you observed William Clement on the bed. When the parties reassembled to take depositions did you discover him leave the bed

Answer - I did not I do not know whether he had left the bed or whether he was still there

Question - How long after the parties reassembled about the deposition was it that you saw James Clement on the bed

Answer - I can't possibly say

Question - State what occurred on the application to adjourn the deposition before the recess

Answer - As well as I recollect, Capt. Witcher moved the court to adjourn over the taking of the depositions until the next week, perhaps Monday, I am not certain about that, alleging as reasons therefor, that he was an old man and was some distance from home, and had been here several days and was anxious to go home that evening. I think Ralph A. Clement objected to the adjournment on the ground that he had a female witness here that had been there three days, and was anxious that the deposition should proceed, I think. I can't give their language exactly. I stepped up and remarked that that was a matter addressed to the sound legal discretion of the court, taking into consideration the circumstances on both sides. James Clement, nor William

Clement neither, said one word as I recollect. I was fearful that Capt. Witcher and Ralph would get excited and I wished to keep off anything of the sort

Question - Did not Vincent Witcher make and maintain his application with the utmost decorum

Answer - I think he did it in a polite, & respectful way upon the first motion

Question - Did he not turn to you and solicit your opinion for the use of the magistrate in deciding his application

Answer - No, not that I recollect of. He did ask my opinion on another matter, for the benefit of the court or justice I gave my opinion in his, Capt. Witcher"s favor, as I believed legally and justly

Question - While the above application was pending did not Ralph Clement say that he asked no favors and could grant none

Answer - I can"t say positively, but I have an impression that words to the import was used by Ralph Clement

Question - What was the color of the chair on which Ralph Clement was sitting at the table when you last saw him

Answer - I don"t recollect to have noticed either the color or the size of the chair, and would not know it if I were to see it

Question - In making your supposition, before stated, of the ability of Vincent Witcher to have made the marks on the chair with a pistol, when you last saw Ralph Clement was his chair so presented to the supposed Vincent Witcher as to enable him to strike it in the manner you stated it was stricken

Answer - If the chair occupied the position when stricken by the bullet that it did when I last saw Ralph Clement sitting on it, it could not have been a bullet from Vincent Witcher"s pistol if he were where I last saw him from the range of the ball

Question - Do you know whether the chair you state was stricken, was that occupied by Ralph Clement when you left the room, or by Vincent Witcher

Answer - I do not know anything about it

Question - Was not Ralph Clement when you last saw him, in the chair *setting* square up to the table to do writing

Answer - My recollection is, that he was *setting* near the table with the corner pointing to his right side, so that if writing, he would have been writing nearly across the end of the table. I mean the remote left hand corner of the table from the magistrate, I don't remember, but am inclined to think that his back was to the back of the chair

Question - You have stated that last fall you saw James Clement *practicising* with a pistol. What time of the fall and where was it

Answer - I believe it was the latter part of November, at James Clement's house

Question - State the parties to the suit in which the depositions before mentioned were taken

Answer - Victoria A. Clement by John Anthony Smith, her next friend, plaintiff against James R. Clement

Question - Was not the object of the defendant's testimony taken during a part of the time, to prove that Vincent Witcher, by bullying and tampering with a witness caused him to give false testimony

Answer - I so understood it

Question - During the several days of the taking of said depositions, in the morning and evenings of the said days, was there not a great deal of firing and practicing with pistols by the deceased parties

Answer - No pistol was fired either in the morning or evening of any day during the taking of the depositions within my knowledge, by any or either of the deceased parties

Question - During those nights

Answer - I *staid* with Ralph A. Clement every night except Saturday night

Question - Where did James and William Clement stay

Answer - William went with me to Ralph's every night. James said he was going home. I know not where he went

Question - With whom did Betsy Bennett come to the place of taking the depositions each day, and who furnished her the means of coming

Answer - She came each day with Ralph A. Clement, Mrs. Shelton, William Clement and myself. It seems to me that we got in company with James on one of the days. She rode a gray mare said to belong to Ralph A. Clement

Question - Had not William Clement recently returned to this neighborhood from the West where he had been residing for *sometime*. If so, when did he return

Answer - He came home to father''s last November or December while I was down there, from Pike''s Peak, as he said

Question - Did he intend to return

Answer - He was making preparations to return as he informed me

Question - Was not the law suit of which you have spoken a subject of deep feeling among the parties to it, and their immediate connections, and of an implacable feud between Vincent Witcher and his near relations and the deceased and their near relations

Answer - So far as I am informed it was a subject of deep feeling among all.

BENJAMIN F. COOPER, J.P.

Adjourned till tomorrow morning, 9 o''clock.

Saturday Morning, March 3d, 1860. Court met pursuant to adjournment same justice as on yesterday

CROSS *EXAMINE* OF SAME WITNESS

Question by counsel for *defence* - At the second application for the continuance do you remember Ralph Clement saying, "I am not responsible for what I say"

Answer - I do not recollect it

Question - During the recess where were the deceased and who was along with them

Answer - They were a good portion of the time together with myself eating a snack in the road on some garden or fence post. After we dispersed from there I have no recollection where they were. If any other person was along I have no recollection of it

Question - When did you reach the neighborhood

Answer - I reached Dr. Clement''s on Saturday night before Pittsylvania court on the following Monday, the last court

Question - Had not you and your wife visited this neighborhood sometimes during last fall or winter, and did she come with ___ {sic} at the present visit

Answer - We visited this neighborhood towards the latter part of last November she did not accompany me on this visit I left her at home

Question - When did you first gain information that depositions were to be taken in the suit

Answer - On Saturday before the first Monday in February, about one o"clock of that day, in the road between Gravely"s store and Henry court-house

Question - Who gave you that information

Answer - Charles J. Clement

Question - Was his business in seeing you to give you that information

Answer - No. He was on his way to North Carolina on other business, as he informed me

Question - Did the deceased parties die intestate

Answer - Ralph A. Clement left a will

Question - When was that will made

Answer - It was made sometime last September, I think

Question - When did you first learn of the existence of that will

Answer - I believe the first time I heard anything about it was in his *dieing* declarations

Question - Did Ralph Clement have on his overcoat when you first approached him, after the firing ceased

Answer - He had on a brown coat that I took to be his overcoat. My impression is that he had on a dark coat under it

Question - Was his will wholly in his handwriting and unattested

Answer - It purports to be so

Question - Are you not a practicing attorney

Answer - I suppose I am. I am doing but little practice now. I have done a great deal

EXAMINATION IN CHIEF RESUMED.

Question by counsel for *commonwealth* - How long did Capt. Witcher pause after the lie was given

Answer - I cannot say – but few minutes I suppose perhaps, some two or three. I was walking slowly out of the room

Question - Did you observe Capt. Witcher in that pause to look around him

Answer - I did not my back being turned towards Capt. Witcher

Question - After shaking your head at Ralph Clement, did he use any insulting language to Capt. Witcher

Answer - Not a word that I heard

Question - Why were you armed on that occasion

Answer - I can't say why, unless in case a difficulty should arise, I would be able to protect myself, and protect others I thought it my duty to protect

Question - Did you see arms or signs of arms on Capt. Witcher or any of the prisoners, or of any of his relations and friends on that day, or during the taking of the depositions

Answer - I saw the hilt or handle of what I took to be a bowie-knife in the breast of Addison Witcher. I saw no other arms. I observed an enlargement about the hip or side of Mr. John A. Smith

Question - Who pointed it out

Answer - James R. Clement

Question - On what day was that

Answer - I cannot say on what day it was during the taking of the depositions

Question - You stated that part of the room where James Clement lay was considerably darkened by the smoke. Was it so dark that you could not distinctly see the arm of the person who fired at him when he was down

Answer - It was not so dark but what I distinctly saw the arm of some person extended towards him with a pistol in his hand, and I saw the blaze from the pistol when discharged

Question - Did the body of Mr. James R. Clement in any manner show the effect of the fire

Answer - I saw not the slightest notion of the body occasioned thereby

Question - Do you know whether Jas. Clement was *lieing* upon the bed when Capt. Witcher took his seat by it

Answer - I do not. I know now which took their positions first.

Question - Had you seen Mr. James Clement at any time during the taking of the depositions, before the second altercation about the continuance, *lieing* on the bed

Answer - I think I had

Question - Did you see Mr. William Clement and either of the Mr. Smiths speaking together that day, or during the day of the depositions

Answer - I did. They spoke near the edge of the porch at Mr. Dickinson"s store

Question - In what manner did they apparently speak to each other

Answer - I took it they spoke friendly

Question - What was Capt. Witcher"s manner, when after the recess he renewed his motion to postpone taking of the depositions. Was it entirely decorous to all the opposite parties, or did it indicate any feeling

Answer - At first, when he made the motion, I looked upon his manner as decorous to the opposite party and to all others. But when he made the remark that I have stated before, about the witness being left in the hands of the opposite party I regarded that as indecorous if not insulting - I mean his language

Question - For whom was his language obviously intended

Answer - I can"t say unless it was for Ralph Clement

Question - Do you know the position of the chair in which Mr. Ralph Clement was *setting* at the time you heard the first fire

Answer - I do not

Question - Could you have seen Ralph A. Clement"s face if the back of the chair had been turned to the petition wall, at the time you shook your head at him

Answer - That depends much upon the fact of what position he occupied upon the chair

Question - When you last saw Mr. Ralph Clement state as near as you can whether he was fronting directly to Capt. Witcher or sitting rather with his side to him

Answer - As I stated before I do not distinctly recollect the position of the body, the only distinct recollection I have is that he looked me in the when I shook my head at him

Question - In the suit of which you have spoken was it not the effort on both sides to discredit the other as much as possible apparently

Answer - From the allegations of the bill and the response of the answer I am led to the conclusion that it was

131

Question - Did you ever see or hear Mr. Ralph A. Clement in any manner, attempt to tamper with the witness Betsy Bennett, about to be sworn

Answer - I never did

Question - Why did you come to Doctor Clement on your last visit

Answer - I had received two letters from John Clement desiring me to come down to attend to some business for him at the next Pittsylvania court

Question - Were you ever invited in any form, by way of the Messrs. Clement, to be present to participate in any combat

Answer - I never was by any one of them

Question - What was the condition of Mr. Ralph A. Clement"s health, generally, during last summer and fall, and to the time of his death

Answer - I can"t say, except from information from himself. On Sunday night previous to last Pittsylvania court, he informed that he was very sick all night and was too unwell to go to court next day and from information derived from him, his health was not very good at any time since the last summer and fall. I have heard him reportedly say that he hadn"t enjoyed good health since his return from Mississippi several years ago

Question - Did you ever know, or have reason to believe, that he had made a previous will to the one of which you spoke

Answer - I do not know the fact, never having seen a previous will

The witness here desired to say that in making his statement in regard to the side of the chair which was stricken by the bullet, he made a mistake by saying that it was stricken on the second slat near the right hand post of the chair, and ranged through the bottom and came out and glanced the left hand front post of the chair when in truth it struck the second slat near the left hand back-post ranged through the bottom of the chair, and came out glancing the right hand front-post on the inner side

CROSS EXAMINATION RESUMED

Question by counsel for *defence* - Were you looking at Vincent Witcher while he was using the language that you considered indecorous

Answer - I do not think I was

M.D. CARTER.

DEPOSITION OF GEORGE T. BERGER

George T. Berger being called and sworn, says

Question by counsel for *commonwealth* - Do you know of any practicing with pistols by either of the Messrs. *Smith's* within the last few weeks

Answer - I have heard shooting towards Mrs. Smith"s but I don"t know who it was by

Question - On how many occasions did you hear it

Answer - I heard it on several, I don"t recollect how many

Question - From the character of the firing did it seem to be from five-shooters or revolvers

Answer - I would ___ {sic} it was from one or the other from the rapid succession of the firing

Question - Do these young gentlemen John A. and Vincent O. Smith reside with Mrs. Smith *there* mother

Answer - I think that Vincent O. did, but don"t think that John A. did

Question - Did you ask one or the other or both of these gentlemen what so such shooting over that way meant

Answer - I don"t recollect ever having asked the question

Question - Did you ever hear either or both of them say why they had been shooting so much in that direction

Answer - I never did.

Question - Do you know when John A. Smith came to his mother"s

Answer - I don"t

Question - In what business is he engaged in Danville

Answer - I don"t know.

CROSS EXAMINATION

Question by counsel for *defence* - About the time you have just spoken, did you hear similar firing from the direction of any of the *deceased* residence

Answer - I did. I have heard firing towards Ralph Clement"s and have also heard firing towards James Clement"s

Question - State the age of John and Oliver Smith

Answer - I would suppose John was twenty and Oliver eighteen

Question - State how long you have known them

Answer - I have known them for the last ten years

Question - Within that time, how far have you resided from them

Answer - I have resided within the last eight or nine years, within a mile or mile-and-a-half of their mother

Question - State if you know their general character for mildness and amiability down to the time of this occurrence. If you do, state it

Answer - I do I think their character for mildness and amiability is as good as any young men I ever knew

Question - State their *connexion* with Vincent Witcher

Answer - *Thay* are grandsons of Capt. Witcher

Question - State the *connexion* of the other defendants with Vincent Witcher

Answer - Addison Witcher is the son of Vincent Witcher, and Samuel Swanson is the son-in-law

Question - State the connection of John and Oliver Smith to Victoria C. Clement

Answer - They are brothers to her

Question - Is the father of the said *Smith's* living If not how long had he been dead

Answer - He is not living he has been dead I think ten years in May next

EXAMINATION IN CHIEF RESUMED

Question by counsel for *commonwealth* - How far do you live from Ralph Clement"s

Answer - I suppose between a quarter and a half mile

Question - Do you know of his having been absent on a trip to North Carolina for some time previous to the difficulty

Answer - I understood he was absent from home

Question - How far do you live from Mr. James Clement"s

Answer - I would suppose it was between two and three miles the way we travel in a direct line it would not be so far his home is in sight of mine

Question - Is not the suit of Mrs. Victoria Clement against her husband brought in the name of Mr. John Smith as her next friend

Answer - I have understood so I don"t know the fact

Question - Do you not think it highly probable, from what you say you have understood, that you are mistaken in supposing John A. Smith to be only twenty years of age

Answer - I may be mistaken as to his being only twenty years of age he may be more than twenty

Question - Do you know whether or not, it has been the habit of either John A. or Vincent O. Smith, of late to carry weapons

Answer - I do not

    GEO. T. BERGER

Adjourned until Monday morning 10 o"clock.

    Benj. F. Cooper, J.P.

DEPOSITION OF JOHN M. HUTCHERSON

Monday, March 5th, 1860. Court met pursuant to adjournment same justice as on yesterday

John M. Hutcherson, being called and sworn, says:

Question by counsel for *commonwealth* - Were you in the room when the firing commenced

Answer - I was

Question - State all you saw and know about it

Answer - About all I do know is that I was in the room at the time

CROSS EXAMINATION

Question by counsel for *defence* - Did you see Vincent Witcher fire the first shot

Answer - I did not

Question - Where were you standing

Answer - Fronting of the fire-place I suppose some six feet off

Question - In what direction were you looking when the first fire was made

Answer - I was looking right at Capt. Witcher at the time

EXAMINATION RESUMED IN CHIEF

Question by counsel for *commonwealth* - Can you undertake to say who did fire the first shot

Answer - I cannot

Question - Did you see Capt. Witcher rise from his seat

Answer - I did

Question - State his manner and all you saw him do

Answer - He *ris* and brought his hand up to his breast as he rose. I didn''t see anything unfriendly about his manner

Question - Did you not upon seeing Capt. Witcher rise {and} leave the room very quickly

Answer - I did it was from seeing Mr. Ralph Clement rise about the same time

Question - Do you know what position James and William Clement occupied at the time the taking of depositions was resumed

Answer - William Clement was lying on the bed the last time I noticed him I know nothing of James'' position

CROSS EXAMINATION RESUMED

Question by counsel for the *defence* - State in what part of the room you were when the first pistol fired

Answer - About the centre of the room I suppose

Question - State the manner in which Ralph Clement arose

Answer - I did not think it was friendly

Question - Why did you think it was unfriendly

Answer - From the language he made use of in rising

Question - State what the language was

Answer - He said "that any person that *saied* that we had the witness in charge tells a lie"

Question - Was it immediately after that that Vincent Witcher arose in the manner you have stated

Answer - It was

Question - In leaving the room, did you last see Vincent Witcher or Ralph Clement

Answer - I saw them both about the same time

Question - Have you stated all you saw of Ralph Clement at the time he arose

Answer – I have

EXAMINATION IN CHIEF RESUMED

Question by counsel for *commonwealth* - Did you leave the room immediately upon seeing Ralph A. Clement rise

Answer - I started about that time to leave the room

Question - Did you observe anything that occurred between Ralph A. Clement and Capt. Witcher after you started to leave the room

Answer - I did not

Question - What language had Capt. Witcher used, that caused Mr. Ralph A. Clement to apply the lie to any person who used it

Answer - Capt. Witcher asked Squire Mitchell to postpone taking of the depositions until another day. Mr. Ralph A. Clement wished to continue taking the depositions, unless the witness was placed under guard or in custody. I don't recollect which. Capt. Witcher said that he was willing that she should be placed in the hands of Ralph A. Clement as they had her in charge. Mr. Clement said she should not be placed in his hands, and any person that said that we have had her in our control tells a lie

JOHN M. HUTCHERSON

EXAMINATION IN CHIEF OF WITNESSES

DEPOSITION OF CHARLES POWELL

Charles Powell being called and more says:

That on Saturday the 26th of last month, I was in the counting-room at Dickinson"s store where they were taking depositions. Betsy Bennett was introduced as a witness. I think it was between twelve and one o"clock, though I am not certain as to the hour. Capt. Witcher requested the magistrate to postpone the taking of the depositions until Monday or *some time* next week, alleging as a reason they could not get through the taking of the depositions that evening. Ralph Clement objected to postponing it. The magistrate decided that he would go on with the taking of the depositions. They then took a recess for dinner. They returned from dinner and the magistrate took his seat. Capt. Witcher again moved for a postponement of the taking of the depositions, urging that he did not think it would be right or just to the parties to commence taking the deposition when they would not be able to complete it that day, leaving the witness in the hands or care of one of the parties, after questions and answers had been given for some days. Ralph Clement said that the witness could be put under guard if they *choosed* it. Capt. Witcher"s reply to that, was that he didn"t know that he had any such right if he had he shouldn,t exercise it. I think Capt. Witcher"s expression was that they had had the witness under their care or charge, I forget which. Ralph Clement then made some expression that I did not distinctly understand. Capt. Witcher replied make your charge more definite or direct, I don"t recollect which there seemed to be a short pause for a second or two. I saw Capt. Witcher and Ralph Clement both rise upon their feet. I then believed there would be a combat. I immediately turned my back upon them and aimed to make my escape out of the room. The whole crowd seemed to be moving toward the door. I made my way to the door as fast as I could. Just before I got to the door I heard a pistol fire in my rear, I did not know who fired it. Before I cleared the door there was two or three other pistols fired in quick succession, and then the firing was very rapid at first towards the end of the combat were not so frequent, and shortly the firing instantly ceased. After the firing had ceased I saw Capt. Witcher and Addison Witcher and Samuel Swanson, John A. Smith and Oliver Smith all coming out of the counting-room into the porch. John A. Smith had a bowie-knife in hand. He paused *near by* me, his coat on fire on his right shoulder. I brushed out the fire with my own hand. There was three bullet-holes in his coat. I examined them and I discovered that two of the holes *was* made with the same bullet but it did not touch the flesh. I think the other bullet went into the shoulder, passed through to the front side of the arm and lodged near the surface. I saw it taken out. Oliver Smith passed on by me also. He appeared to be holding his arm. He left there and came on towards Brook"s with the rest of the company. After they had left I returned to the counting-room where the combat had taken place. On entering the counting-room by the door leading from the store-room to the counting-room, I saw James R. Clement lying dead. His head near the door leading into the store out of the counting- room his feet extended towards the bed he lying on his back a little inclined to the right his face turned to the right so that the side of his face same near the floor there was a considerable pool of blood by his side and from his appearance seemed to be *severly* wounded in the breast he was lying with his right hand across his breast, with the hilt of a bowie-knife grasped in his hand – the bowie-knife was in the scabbard. I thi8nk there was a five-shooter lying near his side. After viewing him, I saw William Clement lying on the floor some little distance from him, perhaps about the middle of the room. He was also dead. One eye appeared to be shot out, the ball entering the outside corner of his eye. I didn't at that time discover any other wound, but this breast was a little bloody the eye that was shot was smartly stained with powder, or powder- burnt. I then turned my eyes to Ralph Clement. He was complaining very much and down upon the floor. I can't say whether he was lying or rather crumpled up, getting with his hands on the floor. Colo. Carter and some other gentlemen were in the room at the time. We took him off of the floor and aid him upon the bed. I discovered when we laid him on the bed that there was two bullet holes in the back of his right shoulder, I think his head was bleeding. I think, from the cut of a glancing ball - which side I cannot now say. After lying upon the bed a while complaining greatly of his back, Carter pulled up his *cloths*. I saw a bullet-hole in the right side of the spine. From the appearance of the bullet-hole and its apparent direction I thought it likely that it had fractured the right kidney. I think he lingered something like two hours and died

Question by counsel for *defence* - While Vincent Witcher was urging his motion for a continuance, state whether or not he kept his seat or arose

Answer - He kept his seat

Question - State whether or not, when Ralph Clement first replied to Vincent Witcher, he kept his seat

Answer - I don't recollect seeing him rise at that time

Question - State whether or not, after the words were passed, which you say you did not distinctly understand, Vincent Witcher and Ralph Clement arose instantly together

Answer - They didn't rise until after Capt. Witcher said "make your charge more definite or direct", and I think, they both arose nearly together

Question - What was your position in the room

Answer - I was *setting* near the *centre* of the room, near the partition wall

Question - State which of the parties you then saw, and where

Answer - Capt. Witcher, when he was *setting* by the side of the bed near the fire-place. Ralph Clement was *setting* near the table on which they were taking of the table near the fire-place. I think the magistrate was at the end of the table near the fire-place, at the east end of the room. Addison Witcher was standing on the opposite side of the table from Ralph Clement near the fire-place, the time I turned to go out, I don't recollect noticing Addison Witcher. As to the other parties, I do not recollect seeing any of them

Question - What was Addison Witcher doing when you last saw him

Answer - I think he was standing up against the wall, or near the wall

140

Question - Was there any obstruction between you, Addison Witcher and the persons about the table

Answer - At times, I think there was. I was *setting* down and persons pausing between could cause obstruction sometimes I could not see Ralph Clement

Question - State as near as you can, the length of time between your leaving to go out, and your seeing Addison Witcher, so you have stated

Answer - I cannot say how long, but not more than a few minutes

Question - Was he so standing, during the above conversation between Vincent Witcher and Ralph Clement

Answer - He was, I think, standing when conversation was going on about the postponement it is more a matter of impression with me than a certainty, at what time precisely, he was standing there

Question - State whether Oliver Smith and Samuel Swanson were wounded. If so, where

Answer - Oliver Smith was wounded near the left *rist* by a pistol-ball on the back part of the arm. Samuel Swanson had a slight wound on one of his arms, I don't recollect which, apparently __ {sic} with a ball

Question - When you approached Ralph Clement did he have any arms about him

Answer - I can't say - I didn't see any. He had a belt around him. I saw Colo. Carter take it off

Question - If you are acquainted with the age of Vincent Witcher, state it

Answer - I think that agreeable to what he had told me, he is upwards of seventy years of age I think he is seventy-one years of age

Question - Did you see Colo. Carter during the words that you have mentioned as passing between Vincent Witcher and Ralph Clement and, if so, where was he

Answer - I think I did he passed near me when I was *setting* and think he spoke to Ralph Clement, and I think his words were, "that ain't the way to do business".

Question - State what reply, if any, Ralph Clement made

Answer - I heard no reply

Question - Had not Ralph Clement been a practicing lawyer

Answer - I think years ago he practiced some in Franklin court. If he practiced anywhere else, I do not know it

CROSS EXAMINATION

Question by counsel for *commonwealth* - On the day of the fight had not Addison Witcher been conducting the examination of testimony on the part of Mrs. Victoria Clement

Answer - He had

Question - When you saw John A. Smith with the gun in his hand - the *reencounter* was it not bloody

Answer - It was stained with blood

Question - You speak of bullet-holes in the clothes of John A. Smith and Samuel Swanson. How many bullet-holes and cuts were there upon the dead bodies of the deceased

Answer - I couldn"t say how many. I saw but one cut. I didn"t examine the bodies. The cut was in the side of William Clement just below the ribs – a pretty severe cut, the intestines protruded out a little

Question - Did you see Samuel Swanson that day, before or after the combat, carrying a stick

Answer - I did see him carrying a stick before and after the combat

Question - When you first saw the stick, before the combat, was it broken or *shivered*

Answer - I think not

Question - The first time you saw it after the combat was it broken or *shiverd*

Answer - The small end was broken off and *shivered*, the first time I saw it after the combat

Question - How long after the combat before you first saw it, and who had it

Answer - I saw it the evening after the combat and I think it was in the hands of Mr. Swanson

Question - Is not Mr. Swanson a very large and strong man, and was not Mr. James Clement a small and delicate man

Answer - Mr. Swanson is a large man, and looks as if he might be a strong man. James Clement was a small man. I think he was an active, athletic small man

Question - Did you observe the position of Mr. Ralph A. Clement in his chair at the time of the altercation about the adjournment of the taking of the deposition

Answer - I saw him *setting* in his chair with his face towards the magistrate, and the magistrate was *setting* near the wall

Question - When Capt. Witcher arose up how far, as near as you can guess, do you suppose he was from the chair on which Clement was *setting*

Answer - I couldn"t say, but suppose it to be from seven to ten feet

Question - You have stated that Ralph Clement was *setting* with his face fronting the justice. Was not his side, therefore, presented to Capt. Witcher

Answer - I think his side must have been rather obliquely to Capt. Witcher

Question - Obliquely to the front or rear

Answer - I think to the front

EXAMINATION IN CHIEF RESUMED

Question by counsel for *defence* - Was Vincent Witcher aiding in taking the examination of the witnesses

Answer - I did not discover that he was

Question - Was Ralph Clement *setting* at the side or end of the table

Answer - I think he was *setting* rather at the corner of the table

CHARLES POWELL

143

DEPOSITION OF CLUFFEE M. BROOKS

Cluffee M. Brooks being called and sworn says:

Question by counsel for the *commonwealth* - State whether you were here or not on the day of the combat and, if so, state all you know about _____ {sic}

Answer - I was at Dickinson"s on that day not in the house at the time

Question - State if you saw anybody after the fight coming out of the counting-room with weapons of any sort about them

Answer - I was standing some fifteen steps from the end of the porch. I saw no person that was said to be in the affray but one of the young Mr. Smiths. He was in the west end of the porch when I saw him and he had a bowie-knife in his hand

Question - Was it bloody

Answer - It appeared bloody to me at the distance I was of it

      CLUFFIE M. BROOKS

CHARLES POWELL BEING RECALLED SAYS:

Question by counsel for *defence* - From what part of the room did the report of the first pistol come and what was there

Answer - The report seemed to come from the north-east corner of the room and the bed was in that part of the house

Question by counsel for *commonwealth* - Was not Capt. Witcher"s chair against the bed or very near it

Answer - It was

Question - Do you undertake to state that report *come* from off the bed

Answer - No, I don"t

CHARLES POWELL

DEPOSITION OF GEORGE FINNEY

George Finney being called and sworn, says:

Question by counsel for *defence* - State if you ever had any conversation with Elizabeth Bennett upon the subject of this prosecution. If so state what it was

Answer - I did, on the evening of the 25th of last month, concerning this *fracus*. She stated to me she did not know who fired the first pistol. The first she knew the firing commenced. It excited her so she slipped under the writing desk. Afterwards she went *up stairs*. Immediately after it was all over she hurried off

Question - To whom did she direct this conversation

Answer - To myself

Question - Did she ask you if you knew who did the first firing

Answer - She did not

Question - Were you at the shooting

Answer - I was here on the ground, but not present

Question - State if you heard the first and last fire

Answer- I did

Question - Where were you at the first fire whether or not you proceeded towards the firing, and how far you got when it ended

Answer - I was in the road that leads to Snow Creek about one hundred and twenty-five yards, at least, almost the time I get to the west end of the porch

Question - Did you or not afterwards measure the distance

Answer - I did
Question - In what pace did you go

Answer - I ran pretty fast.

Question- Are you a fast runner

Answer - I am as fast as common, I *recon*

146

Question - How old are you

Answer - I was nineteen the ninth day of last December

Question - Where did the above conversation with Betsy Bennett occur

Answer - At Ralph Clement"s

CROSS EXAMINATION

Question by counsel for *commonwealth* - How long after the fight before you saw Betsy Bennett

Answer - I can"t tell exactly about an hour *and-a-half*

Question - Were you not both of you very much excited

Answer - I can"t speak for her. I was excited

Question - Did she speak in a loud voice

Answer - She did not very

Question - Why did she make these statements to you

Answer - I can"t tell more than that I was anxious to know. I asked the question

Question - Did you see her at Dickinson"s the day of the fight

Answer - I did

Question - Why did you ask her the question about who began it

Answer - Because I was anxious to know who began it, and knew she was here and expected she was in the room at the time it began

Question - Did you ever see her before that day

Answer - I saw her on Thursday before the first time

Question - Did you ever speak to her or she to you

Answer - I don"t know as she ever did, nor I to her

Question - Why did you go down to Ralph Clement"s that evening

Answer - At the request of Mrs. Dickinson. I went down after Ralph Clement"s wife

Question - Was Ralph Clement living or dead when you left

Answer - He was living

Question - When you got there did not his family and the persons there gather around you to hear the news of his condition

Answer - His wife did, had no other person

Question - Who else was at his house when you got there

Answer - Mastin Williams and his, Ralph Clement"s, overseer, and some ladies didn"t know who they were

Question - Who was present when Betsy Bennett made the statement to you *you* have stated above

Answer - No person as I recollect of very close there were persons passing about

Question - Did she take you one side to make this statement, and did she do it in a low voice

Answer - She did not she did it in the door

Question - Were you on the inside of the door or the outside

Answer - I was standing against the facing of the door inside

Question - Where was Betsy Bennett standing then

Answer - She was standing on the opposite side of the door inside

Question - Was the room that door lead into a large one

Answer - I think it was a passage that that door led into

Question - Who was in the passage

Answer - No person that I recollect of, more than passing through

Question - Who passed through

Answer - Mrs. Clement and one or two other ladies that I didn"t know passed up stairs

Question - Do you undertake to say now that you do not know the names of any of the ladies there then, except that of Mrs. Clement, either by your own knowledge or from others

Answer - I do not. I never heard any person say who they were except as to Mrs. Clement, and Miss Bennett

Question - How long have you and Betsy Bennett is conversation in the door

Answer - I cannot tell I suppose four or five minutes

Question - You have stated that Mastin Williams and Ralph Clement"s overseer were there. Where were they whilst this conversation between you and Elizabeth Bennett was going on

Answer - Mastin Williams had gone off his overseer was passing about. I can"t tell where he was while the conversation was going on. I could see him, though, frequently passing about

Question - Do you mean to say that you saw Clement"s overseer frequently while you and Betsy Bennett were talking in the door

Answer - I mean to say that I saw him frequently while I was there. I saw him once or twice while we were in conversation passing by

Question - State as near as you can where he was when you saw him during the conversation

Answer - He paused by the door once or twice while the conversation was going on. I saw him once go to the blocks but whether this was while the conversation was going on I can"t say

Question - What is the overseer"s name

Answer - I understand his name is Huffman. I have heard him called by that name. I am not acquainted with him

Question - Did Betsy Bennett have her bonnet on while you and her were in conversation

Answer - I think she did

Question - As you had seen her once before and known her so slightly, might you not have mistaken her for her sister about the same size and with only a year or two difference in their ages

Answer - No I am confident it was her. I recognized her bonnet and dress that I have seen her have on an hour or two before here

Question - What sort of dress did she have on here

Answer - I think it was a striped dress. I don"t know what kind of goods it was

Question - What kind of bonnet

Answer - I think it was a red striped bonnet

Question - Were the dress and the bonnet you speak of the same she had on her while standing in the door making these disclosures to you

Answer - I think they were

Question - Did you speak to her when you first saw her on that day

Answer - I did not

Question - Were you introduced at Clement"s the day you went down there

Answer - I was not

Question - As you did not speak to her on Thursday, and was not introduced to her on the evening you went there after Mrs. Clement, how could she have known who you were

Answer - I can"t tell

Question - Did she call you by name

Answer - She did not

Question - How did the prisoners know that Betsy Bennett and you had ever had this conversation

Answer - I told it to some person and they informed them of it, and sine I told it to them

Question - Where did say you were when the firing began

Answer - I said I was on the Snow Creek road about one hundred and twenty-five or thirty yards off

Question - Who was with you

Answer - John Baker and Tom Keen

Question - Why did you measure the distance from where you was to the store

Answer - By the request of Addison Witcher

EXAMINATION IN CHIEF RESUMED

Question by counsel for *defence* - State if you are related to the widow of Ralph Clement and if so, in what degree

Answer - I am first cousin

Question - On the occasion of the above conversation, did you hear Mrs. Clement address Miss Bennett by any name

Answer - I did not as I recollect of

Question - State if in any way Mrs. Clement identified said Miss Bennett

Answer - She did. She said the Witchers were determined not to let Miss Betsy Bennett"s deposition be taken. I thought she was alluding to this woman

EXAMINATION RESUMED

Question by counsel for *commonwealth* - What was the color of the dress she had on at Dickinson"s store where you saw her an hour and a half before the conversation alluded to

Answer - I think it a red and white striped dress

EXAMINATION IN CHIEF RESUMED

Question by *defence* - Did you hear Elizabeth Bennett give her evidence in this case

Answer - I did not

Question - Did you see her before the magistrate to be examined as a witness on the day of the shooting

Answer - I saw her in the presence of the magistrate

Question - Was she the same person as that with whom you held the above conversation

Answer - I think she was

Question - Who went with you to see Mrs. Clement

Answer - John B. Law

GEORGE W. FINNEY

DEPOSITION OF ROBERT N. POWELL

Robert N. Powell, being called and sworn, says:

That I was at Dickinson"s store on the 25th day of last month and was present at the time Capt. Witcher moved for an adjournment of the taking of the depositions till the next week or Monday said that he lived some piece off and wished to go home that evening. Mr. Ralph A. Clement objected to his motion and said he had a female witness there and the magistrate decided to go on taking the depositions. The magistrate then granted a recess for dinner. After they had got back, Capt. Witcher removed his motion and said that he didn"t think it justice to commence the taking of the deposition when it was not likely to be completed on that day, and leave the witness in the hands of the parties, or the other party. I *aint* certain which. Ralph Clement remarked that she could be put under guard. Capt. Witcher said he didn"t know that he had any such right, and if he did he wouldn"t exercise it, and remarked something about her being in the hands of the other party, or *some thing* about her being dictated to and being prepared to answer questions that might be put to her afterwards. When Capt. Witcher said that she was in the hands of the other party, Ralph Clement said, "the man that told that told a lie, or a damned lie", I don"t recollect which I think a damned lie though. Capt. Witcher remarked, "make your charge more definite or direct". There was a moment"s pause and both men *ris* and clapped their hands to their bosoms, as if they intended to draw their weapons. While they were in the act of drawing weapons I heard the report of a pistol, that drew my attention from them. I looked towards where the sound was and saw James Clement upon the bed rather in a crooked condition, as if he was rising, with his pistol presented and the smoke boiling up before his face. My attention was then drawn from him by a scuffle with Ralph A. Clement and Addison Witcher, and pretty quick I saw Samuel Swanson and James Clement engaged - Swanson striking with his stick and Clement firing at him. I looked at them until I heard three fires from James Clement"s pistol. My attention was again drawn to Ralph A. Clement and Addison Witcher saying to *some one* "don"t shoot me - shoot the damned rascal. I then heard the report of a pistol right close by and saw the man that fired ii, I took to be Oliver Smith. I am satisfied that it was him. The next thing I saw was Capt. Witcher with his pistol presented towards James Clement and fired. James Clement fell. I then turned my eye back where Ralph Clement was, and he was sinking down rather on his elbow. I heard him say that he "was a dead - they have killed me for nothing". After leaving the room, I saw John A. Smith with his bowie-knife in his hand with it stained with blood

Question by counsel for *defence* - To whom did Vincent Witcher address his remarks for the continuance and the reasons in support thereof

Answer - To the justice, as I understood him

Question - What was his manner

Answer - He seemed to be perfectly cool and polite in his remarks I thought

Question - State your position in the room

Answer - I was seated on the stair-steps at the time the first conversation commenced. About the time that Capt. Witcher and Clement *ris* I *ris* also and stood upon the steps during the balance of the difficulty

Question - On what steps did you stand

Answer - On the second step from the floor

Question - Did not your position elevate you far above the heads of the others in the room and give you a distinct opportunity of seeing what occurred

Answer - I think I must have been elevated some eighteen inches above the floor, and had a better opportunity than any person I saw to see

Question - Were you composed, or sufficiently so, distinctly to perceive and remember what occurred

Answer - I think I was sufficiently composed to recollect anything I distinctly saw. I think I saw everything that came before my eyes. I was not as much discomposed in the room as I was afterwards

Question - State the position of the magistrate, the table, the witness and of all the parties that took part in the difficulty

Answer - The magistrate was sitting at the table between the table and the jam on the south side of the fire-place, at the east end of the house the witness was sitting at the west end of the table rather facing the magistrate Capt. Witcher was sitting on the opposite side of the fire-place from the magistrate near the bed. Ralph Clement was sitting on the same side of the table with {the} witness near her. Addison Witcher was standing up, as well as I recollect, between the magistrate and the writing-desk rather back behind him. I don"t recollect how any other one of the parties was placed until the fight commenced

Question - Was Vincent Witcher directly opposite the magistrate

Answer - I can"t tell whether he was exactly or not, but he was pretty much opposite I suppose

Question - Was Ralph Clement facing Vincent Witcher

Answer - I don"t think he was. I think his face was rather more towards the magistrate than it was towards Capt. Witcher

Question - On which side was Addison Witcher

Answer - He was east of the table. I don"t know whether it was side or end

Question - How was he standing with reference to the magistrate

Answer - I think he was rather behind the magistrate, rather to the right of him

Question - Did he have his pipe in his mouth

Answer - I don"t recollect whether he did or not

Question - Was the above the position of the parties when Vincent Witcher and Ralph Clement arose

Answer - That"s my impression

Question - What caused the pause

Answer - I don"t know that I can say

Question - Did you observe Vincent Witcher during the pause

Answer - I think I did. He seemed to set still a moment

Question - At that moment who was on the bed

Answer - I don"t recollect of noticing any person on the bed at __ {sic} moment

Question - When Vincent Witcher said "make your remarks more direct" what did Ralph Clement say to it

Answer - I have no recollection of any reply

Question - Did he reply

Answer - Not that I recollect of

Question - Which seemed to start to rise first

Answer - I think they both rose at the same moment

Question - Had they straightened up before the pistol fired

Answer - I think so. I think both *was* straight

Question - Did you see Vincent Witcher take out his pistol

Answer - did not

Question - Did you discover that he had drawn his pistol before the first fire

Answer - I did not

Question - Which did you first observe, the firing of the pistol or Vincent Witcher drawing his pistol

Answer - I heard the fire of the pistol before Vincent Witcher drew his pistol

Question - Did Ralph Clement get out his pistol

Answer - I never saw him have any pistol out

Question - State what he did towards drawing his pistol

Answer - He *ris* and put his hand to his bosom like a man that was aiming to draw weapons

Question - In what way was he seized

Answer - I never saw Witcher when he caught him.

BENJAMIN F. COOPER, J.P.

Adjourned till to-morrow at 9 o'clock.

Thursday morning March 6th, 1860. Court met pursuant to adjournment same justice as on yesterday

EXAMINATION IN CHIEF RESUMED

Robert N. Powell being again called, says:

Question by counsel for *defence* - Did you see him holding him

Answer - I think I did both had hold of each other, is my recollection

Question - State how they held each other

Answer - I don't think I can state exactly how they did have hold of each other

Question - Did they scuffle while they were holding

Answer - They did

Question - During the holding and scuffling on which side of the table were they

Answer - They were on the south side of the table between the table and the window, on the south side of the house

Question - When Addison Witcher proceeded to seize Ralph Clement, where was Addison Witcher standing

Answer - The last I saw of Addison Witcher, before I saw him and Clement engaged, he was standing near the writing-desk on the south side of the fire-place

Question - Was he to the right or left of the magistrate, as the magistrate was sitting

Answer - He was on the left of the magistrate rather behind him

Question - What was the effect of the first fire

Answer - I do not know whether it struck any person or not, or where it struck

Question - Can you state against whom it was aimed

Answer - When I heard the report of the pistol and turned towards where the sound was, the pistol seemed to be directed in the course where Addison Witcher stood

Question - Did Addison Witcher and Clement then have hold of each other

Answer - The first time I saw them after the report of the pistol they did

Question - Did you observe them immediately after the report of the pistol

Answer - They were the first ones I recollect noticing afterwards

Question - Was not Vincent Witcher"s back turned to the bed at the first fire

Answer - I think he was rather with his side to the bed at the first fire

Question - Where was his face directed

Answer - Towards Ralph Clement, at the west side of the magistrate"s table

Question - Did Addison Witcher ease Ralph Clement down when he was shot

Answer - I can"t say whether he did or not

Question - After the firing had continued for some time was it not light comparatively between the two windows and dark in the other parts of the room

Answer - It was much lighter on the south side of the room than it was on the north side

Question - Did you see any part of any weapon about Ralph Clement during the scuffle between him and Addison

Answer - I did not

Question - Did you see any about Addison Witcher

Answer - No, I did not

Question - During the fight did James Clement get back towards the table

Answer - I don't recollect seeing him any nearer the table than the side of the bed

Question - Did you see Colo. Carter during the angry words

Answer - I do not recollect seeing of him

Question - Did you see Samuel Swanson have anything but a stick

Answer - No, the stick was the same as shown on yesterday

CROSS EXAMINATION OF WITNESS

Question by counsel for *commonwealth* - Did you state before the coroner that Ralph A. Clement, in his reply to Capt. Witcher's charge about the witness having been brought there by the opposite party, used the term "damned lie", or "lie"

Answer - I think I stated he used the term "damned lie"

Question - Did Capt. Witcher State in his remarks about said witness, that she had been brought there under the charges of the opposite party, as a fact of his own knowledge, or did he say he had been so informed

Answer - My recollection about it is that Capt. Witcher said she was in the hands of the other party. I don't recollect his saying who she was brought there by

Question - Did you hear Capt. Witcher say anything about tampering with the witness

Answer - I think I heard him say that the witness might be dictated to is my recollection

Question - In your testimony before the coroner did you say anything about any pause on the part of Capt. Witcher

Answer - I don't recollect whether I did or not

Question - Have you forgotten the important facts you swore to before the coroner

Answer - I have not

Question - Did you state in your evidence before the coroner that you saw the smoke from the pistol of James Clement, boiling up from the same, or did you state that the next thing you heard was the report from a pistol that came from near where you saw James Clement

Answer - My recollection is that I stated before the coroner that I heard the report of a pistol turned my eye towards the sound and saw the smoke boiling up or rising before James Clement - or something to that amount

Question - When you saw the smoke boiling up from James Clement"s pistol, how far was he from Vincent Witcher

Answer - If I was not deceived in the position of Capt. Witcher - he was some three or four feet from him

Question - If James Clement had presented his pistol in the attitude of delivering a fire at Capt. Witcher"s body, how far could the muzzle of his pistol have been from Witcher

Answer - Not more than some two or three feet, I would suppose

Question - What was James Clement"s position exactly, and where was he when you saw the smoke from his pistol

Answer - He was standing on the bed in a crooked or rising position, about two feet from the head of the bed

Question - Did the pistol seem to be on a level with James Clement"s hand or did it point up or down, to the right or left

Answer - The muzzle of the pistol seemed to be directed towards the south-east corner of the house in the direction of where Addison Witcher stood, the last time I noticed him before the fire. I cannot say whether it was above or below a level

Question - Standing on the stair-steps facing the door of the front entrance, where was Addison Witcher standing, to your right or your left

Answer - He was standing to my right

Question - How far to the right from a straight line down from yourself to the *centre* of the front door did Addison Witcher stand

Answer - I cannot say exactly how far, but I would suppose that he was some eight or nine feet, may be ten

Question - What is the width of the counting-room where the fight took place from east to west

Answer - I would suppose it was some fourteen or sixteen feet

Question - Did you find any impression of balls beyond where Addison Witcher stood

Answer - I *see* the impression of a ball not far from the direction of where Addison Witcher stood in the ceiling which seemed to strike in an oblique way there is an impression of a ball on the ceiling near the stair-steps where I stood, or it had that appearance

Question - Is not the plank of the ceiling made of paper

Answer - I can''t say whether it is or not
Question - Is not the impression you speak of as being that of a ball so slight as {to} leave you in much doubt about it

Answer - I am inclined to think it is a ball there is some doubt about it

Question - Did you not say that Washington Blunt and Henry C. Mease, on the day of the burial of the dead, that you could not say who fired the first pistol that when you turned your head you saw smoke near him and inferred, therefore, that James Clement fired the first pistol, but that you could not or would not swear it

Answer - I don''t have any recollection of making any such statement as that. I recollect of having a conversation with David W. Blunt, and, I think I said to him when asked by him who fired the first pistol, that I heard a report of a pistol, turned my head, towards the sound, and the smoke was boiling up before James Clement. So far as saying to Mr. Mease I have no recollection of speaking to him at all that day

Question - In the conversation alluded to with David W. Blunt, did you not state to him that you inferred from certain facts that you then mentioned, that James Clement fired the first shot, but that you could not or would not swear it

Answer - I have no recollection of making any such statement as that to him

Question - How many fires had you heard when your attention was first attended to the scuffle between Ralph Clement and Addison Witcher

Answer - I have no recollection of but one

Question - How far was Oliver Smith from Ralph Clement, when he fired upon him, while Addison Witcher had hold of him

Answer - Some three or feet I would suppose

Question - Did Oliver Smith level and aim his pistol deliberately

Answer - He presented his pistol towards Ralph Clement. I can''t say whether he was deliberate about it or not. I think his pistol was aimed at Ralph Clement

Question - Was it about the time that the shot was fired by Oliver Smith, that Ralph Clement cried out, "I am a dead man - they have killed me for nothing"

Answer - It was shortly after that, that I heard him make use of *them* remarks. It was after he had *fell* upon the floor and the firing had ceased

Question - Had any of Ralph"s friends come into the room or gone to him to render him assistance when he made the above remarks

Answer - I think not

Question - Then to whom did he address the remark, "I am a dead man – they have killed me for nothing"

Answer - I am unable to say who, whether he was talking to himself or to whom he addressed it. I didn"t see anybody there to address the remark to

Question - Were the remarks made in a tone of voice that indicated a cry for quarters

Answer - I do not know

Question - How long before the firing ceased did he fall to the floor

Answer - I have no recollection of hearing any firing after I *see* he had fallen

Question - Did you see him in the act of falling

Answer - When I first discovered him I don"t think he was entirely down he was rather down on his elbow. I think he was in the attitude of falling

Question - Did not Addison Witcher say, "shoot the damned rascal but be particular not to shoot me"

Answer - He said, "damn it, don"t shoot me shoot the damned rascal". That is my recollection of what passed

Question - Was Addison Witcher wounded at all in the combat

Answer - I can"t say whether he was or not. I *see* a little skinned place on one of his fingers. I can"t say whether it was there before or not. It was not sufficiently deep to cause it to bleed

Question - Was there not considerable inequality in the size of Addison Witcher and Ralph Clement

Answer - There was a considerable difference in their height and I would suppose Addison Witcher was right smartly the heaviest one

160

Question - When Clement fell what did Addison Witcher do

Answer - I have no recollection of his doing anything else while in the room. I recollect seeing him come out

Question - When you saw Oliver Smith fire at Ralph Clement, while Addison Witcher was holding him, did said Smith prepare his pistol by cocking or otherwise for a second fire at Ralph Clement

Answer - I don"t recollect

Question - Did you at this time cease to observe the man who was firing upon another while he was engaged in a scuffle – a third person of larger size than himself

Answer - I did my attention was drawn off from a fire in a different part of the room

Question - Who delivered that fire   At whom was it shot

Answer - Capt. Witcher was the man fired the pistol and I think it was fired at James Clement

Question - Why do you think it was – fired at James Clement

Answer - Because the pistol was pointed in the direction of where James Clement was, and James Clement falling at the time the pistol fired

Question - Where was James Clement

Answer - He was between the foot of the bed on the north side of the house and the door leading out of the counting-room into the store-room

Question - What was James Clement doing at that time

Answer - I think he was making towards the door

Question - Do you mean to say that Capt. Witcher fired upon him when he was retreating

Answer - I do not know whether he was retreating or not of what purpose he was getting to the door for

Question - Was his front or his back to Capt. Witcher when he received this shot

Answer - I am of the impression that his back was rather towards him

Question - Where was Capt. Witcher when he fired this shot

Answer - He was standing by the side of the bed near the foot

161

Question - How long did the firing continue after the shot from Capt. Witcher, which you say brought James Clement down

Answer - This is the last fire that I recollect

Question - What did Capt. Witcher do with his pistol after firing this shot

Answer - I cannot say

Question - You have described the position of many of the parties engaged in the combat state what position William C. Clement occupied, living and dead

Answer - I have no recollection of seeing William Clement until after the firing had ceased. I started out of the room I saw William Clement lying dead with his feet towards the bed, his head towards the *centre* of the room

Question - Can you account for not seeing William Clement during the fight as you saw so many others

Answer - I cannot say. I do not know how to account for not seeing him

Question - You have stated that you were on the stair-steps during the combat. Was not your position, therefore, such as to give you a full view of every man engaged either with pistols or knives

Answer - I cannot say, for I don't know where they all were.   My position was such that I could see over most of the room

Question - From your position on the stair-steps could you see distinctly the spot upon which Mr. William Clement fell

Answer - I could when there was no obstruction between me and the place where he lay

Question - Did not James Clement and William Clement fall near together

Answer - I suppose their feet was some four feet apart

Question - Which fell nearest to you

Answer - William

Question - Did you not have as good opportunity to see William as James in the fight

Answer - I cannot say, as I did not see William at all while the fight was going on

162

Question - Did you see, on the day of the fight, or say any time during the taking of the depositions, hear or see, William Clement say, or do anything offensive to anybody

Answer - I did not

Question - Did you see him and any of the persons speak in a friendly way to each other

Answer - I have no recollection of seeing him speak to any one of the persons either friendly or unfriendly

Question - State as exactly as you can, where Betsy Bennett was when the magistrate was about to administer the oath to her

Answer - She was *setting* on the west side of the table I think

Question - Was not the west side of the table the furthest off from the fire and the chimney

Answer - I can't answer it exactly, but would suppose it was rather the furthest if anything

Question - You have stated that Ralph A. Clement was in the act of drawing a pistol. What act did he do that made you believe this

Answer - He *ris* and put his hand to his bosom

Question - Do you not know that his pistol was in his belt around his waist and not in his bosom

Answer - I do not know whether it was in his belt or not, or whether he had any belt. I don't know I never saw it

Question - If his arms were in his belt around his waist, did you see him at any time place his hands so as to draw a weapon from that part of his person

Answer - I can't tell

Question - Did you see him place his hands about his waist

Answer - I think *I* was about his waist

Question - Where were you sitting when the altercation occurred about the adjournment of the – {sic} depositions between Capt. Witcher and Dr. Ralph A. Clement

Answer - I was. W was sitting on the lower step of the stairs

Question. Was not your seat lower than the height of an ordinary stair

Answer - It was

Question - Were not a good many persons standing around and about the table where the deposition was about to be taken

Answer - I think there was several

Question - When you saw Oliver Smith shoot Ralph Clement, while Addison Witcher was holding him, was Clement"s face or back to Smith

Answer - I can"t say positively but am inclined to think he was rather side ways to him

Question - Did not the firing, the blood and the falling of the dead and your own great peril, and the cry of Ralph "they have killed me for nothing" greatly agitate you

Answer - I don"t think I was much agitated

Question - Are you related to Capt. Witcher

Answer - I am by marriage my wife is a niece of his

EXAMINATION IN CHIEF RESUMED

Question by counsel for the *defence* - When Vincent Witcher arose did he advance on Ralph Clement

Answer - I think me made a step or two in that direction

Question - Did you observe during the depositions that James Clement had a black sword-cane

Answer - I don"t recollect that I did

Question - Did he have any cane at all If so, describe it

Answer - He had a cane. I think it was a hickory stick of tolerable smart size - a large walking cane. The stick was unvarnished - a white stick

Question - Was there any other fire made on Ralph Clement by Oliver Smith than the one of which you have spoken before Ralph Clement said, "I am a dead man"

Answer - I don"t recollect seeing Oliver Smith make but one fire on him. I suppose from the fact that Addison Witcher said, "damn it don"t shoot me - shoot the damned rascal" that Smith had shot before

Question - Did Addison Witcher say "shoot the damned rascal" after Ralph Clement fell

Answer - It was before. I never heard him say it afterwards

Question - Did Addison Witcher have Ralph Clement around the arms and waist with his arms

Answer - I think not

Question - Was the front door leading into the porch closed all the time

Answer - I do not recollect whether it was or not

Question - Do you know which was the strongest man, Addison Witcher or Ralph Clement

Answer - I do not I know nothing about the strength of either man

Question - Were you requested by Vincent Witcher to be present at the taking of the depositions

Answer - I was not

CROSS EXAMINATION RESUMED

Question by counsel for *commonwealth* - Who was standing on the stair steps with you while the firing was going on

Answer - I have no recollection of any one being on the steps except myself

The court then removed to the room in which the affray occurred, and the following testimony taken in the room. The same witness being further examined, says:

That he does not know whether the table stands precisely now as it stood when the occurrence took place, that the ends of the table might occupy the position the side did on that occasion but that it occupies the same part of the floor, as nearer as he can place it, that it did then. The magistrate was sitting on the west side of the end of the table. Addison Witcher was standing rather to the left and behind the magistrate. The witness was sitting rather to the left and behind the magistrate. The witness was sitting on the west side of the table near the north-west corner. Mr. Ralph Clement was sitting on the same side near the south-west corner

Question - If the magistrate had leaned back in his chair could he not have touched the wall

Answer - I think he could

Question - If he had so touched the wall could Addison Witcher have gotten the position which you said he occupied

Answer - I don"t think he could

Question - Why

Answer - Because if the magistrate had leaned back there could not have been room on account of the desk.

Question - Where was the desk

Answer - It was in the south-east corner of the room, and so near the magistrate that there was not room for Addison Witcher to have gotten between it and the magistrate, and up against the wall so that he couldn't have gotten around it.

Question - Were you armed her on the day of the affray

Answer - I was not

CROSS EXAMINATION

Question by counsel for *commonwealth* - Did you see Addison Witcher leave his position behind the magistrate

Answer - I did not

R.N. POWELL

DEPOSITION OF JOHN B. LAW

John B. Law being called and sworn for *defence* , says:

That I was in the room when they commenced. Mr. Ralph Clement gave Capt. Witcher the lie. Mr. Witcher got up and said something, I couldn't understand him what he said. I saw Mr. James Clement lying on the bed and William Clement, I supposed it to be him after seeing him dead, as I did not know him. James Clement commenced getting up, I saw him draw a pistol. About that time I turned my head and started out. I hadn't got far before I heard the report of a pistol. I turned my head towards Mr. James Clement. I saw him holding his head *sorter* before him, I saw the smoke from the pistol. I think, rising. That was all I saw in the room at that time

Question by the counsel for *defence* - What was Vincent Witcher doing while James Clement was drawing his pistol

Answer - I couldn't see Mr. Witcher's face at that time. I saw him bring his hands up towards his vest about his waist

Question - What was the position of James Clement when you saw him with his arm extended with the pistol in his hand

Answer - He was standing up

Question - Where was he

Answer - He was on the bed

Question - While he was preparing to shoot, what was William Clement doing

Answer - He was getting up. I don't recollect seeing him do anything else after getting up

Question - What did he do after he arose on the bed

Answer - I don't recollect seeing him do anything else after he rose up.

Question - While you observed William Clement on the bed, did he make a motion towards drawing a pistol If so, state what it was

Answer - He put his hands towards his breast

Question - Did you observe whether or not he drew his pistol

Answer - I did not

Question - About the time, or just before that, James Clement drew his pistol, did you or not discover any whispering between him and William Clement

Answer - I did

Question - Did or not James and William Clement rise about the same time from the bed

Answer - I think that James Clement got up first but both started about the same time

Question - Where were you standing

Answer - About two feet or two-and-a-half from the foot of the bed

Question - State whether or not there seemed to be a pause after the first fire

Answer - There did

Question - State if you know what occasioned it

Answer - I do not

Adjourned till to-morrow morning 9 o"clock.

BENJAMIN F. COOPER J.P.

Wednesday morning, March 7th, 1860. Court not pursuant to adjournment same justice as yesterday

CROSS EXAMINATION

John B. Law being recalled, says:

Question by counsel for *commonwealth* - Did you state before the coroner that Mr. Ralph Clement had given Capt. Witcher the lie

Answer - I don"t think I did

Question - Did you state all the facts before the coroner that you have stated here

Answer - I didn"t state everything. He didn"t ask me anything about William Clement

Question - Don"t you distinctly recollect that you were before three inquests and gave evidence with references to the three deceased

Answer - I do not

Question - Do you state that you did not testify with reference to the deaths of Messrs. Ralph, James and William Clement before the coroner

Answer - I testified as to the death of James and Ralph Clement. I don"t recollect about saying anything as to the death of William Clement

Question - Were you not called before the coroner in each of the three cases

Answer - I don"t think I was

Question - When you saw Capt. Witcher and Mr. Ralph Clement rising in the attitude, as you say, of drawing weapons, did you not leave the room, as a large majority of the crowd did, as quick as you could get out

Answer - I didn"t start immediately. As soon as Capt. Witcher arose
Question - State as nearly as {you} can how long it was after Capt. Witcher arose before you did start

Answer - It wasn"t a minute

Question - In that time, which was less than a minute, did you see William and James Clement in a whisper and James rise and present a pistol, and William rise and put his hand to his bosom, as though he was going to draw a weapon and did you see the smoke of James" pistol

Answer - The whispering was going on before this. When James Clement and William Clement commenced rising. I saw Mr. James Clement draw his pistol. I saw the smoke of James" pistol after I had started from the room

Question - Did you see anything else but the smoke of James" pistol, connected with this matter after you had started to leave the room

Answer - I did not

Question - Have you not stated, in the presence of Johnson Clement and John C. Law, that when you saw James Clement and John A. Smith making towards each other, you left the room and saw no more of this affair

Answer - I have not. I have stated before them I heard some person also say so

Question - Who did you tell them said so

Answer - I didn"t know them who said so. A friend of mine told me, and would tell J. C. Law who it was

Question - Did you tell Johnson Clement who it was

Answer - I did not

Question - Did you not tell Johnson Clement and John C. Law that James Clement was on the floor at the foot of the bed when you last saw him

Answer - I did not. I told them that some person had told me that he was at the foot of the bed

Question - Did you tell them who told you so

Answer - I did not

Question - Was there anything remarkable in seeing two brothers whispering, that you should have recollected it so distinctly

Answer - Seeing them whispering was nothing uncommon with friends and brothers. I was asked the questions about their whispering, and answered it on that account

Question - How did the prisoners find out that you knew anything also this whispering

Answer - I didn"t know that any of them were prisoners at that time. I was talking to a friend at that time

Question - To what friends were you talking

Answer - I was talking to Billy Poindexter

Question - Did you suppose that the whispering was as important fact connected with the death of these men

Answer - I thought so

Question - You say that you did not know that they were prisoners at that time, do you not know that a warrant was issued by a justice very soon after the killing for their arrest

Answer - I did not know it until Sunday evening I didn"t know it then but I had heard it

Question - How long before the firing began was it when you saw this whispering
Answer - It was maybe, some three or four minutes

Question - What was the position of James Clement at the time you speak of seeing the smoke from his pistol

Answer - He was standing up, not exactly straight, on the bed

Question - When you say you saw William Clement rising from the bed, had you then heard a fire

Answer - I hadn't heard *narry* one in that room

Question - Were you not leaving the room because you were expecting the firing to begin

Answer - When I did leave I was leaving for that cause

Question - Were you not getting out as rapidly as you could and under excitement

Answer - I was

Question - Did you say anything in your testimony before the coroner about the smoke from James Clement's pistol

Answer - I think I did

Question - Which arose first, Capt. Witcher from his seat, or William Clement, from the bed

Answer - Mr. Witcher got up first

Question - Do you swear that you were in the room when the altercation began between Capt. Witcher and Mr. Ralph Clement, and when the first pistol was fired

Answer - I was in there. Mr. Clement gave Capt. Witcher the lie. I had just got in there, and I was in there when the first pistol was fired

Question - You have stated that the whispering between William and James Clement had taken place about three minutes before you turned to leave. If you had got in, as you say you did, when Ralph gave Capt. Witcher the lie, how did you see the whispering

Answer - I was in the room pretty close to the bed when I saw the whispering, about two or two-and-half feet from the foot of the bed

Question - How did it happen, if you were in the room in time to see the whispering, as you have stated, that you had just got in when you heard Ralph give Capt. Witcher the lie

Answer - Because I didn't think that four or five minutes was much

Question - If you were in there four or five minutes how does it happen that you did not hear what Capt. Witcher said as well as what Mr. Clement said

Answer - When Mr. Clement spoke they all appeared to be tolerable still. When Capt. Witcher spoke there was some of the people trying to get out

Question - Hadn't Capt. Witcher said something when you say Ralph give him the "damned lie"

Answer - I didn't hear him

Question - Then do you state that the first thing you heard or saw, except the well-remembered whispering between James and William Clement was the lie from Ralph to Witcher

Answer - I heard Capt. Witcher say something which I couldn't understand about some depositions I thought. It was not *worth while* for me to say anything about it

EXAMINATION IN CHIEF RESUMED

Question for counsel for *defence* - Did you observe Addison Witcher during your stay in the room If so, where was he

Answer - I didn't know Addison Witcher at the time, but saw a man after it was over, that I supposed to be him. He was tolerable close to the end of the writing-desk, next to the fire-place

Question - In your examination before the coroner state whether or not it was conducted on question and answer

Answer - It was conducted by question and answer

CROSS EXAMINATION

Question by counsel for *commonwealth* - Is this paper exhibited to you a true copy of the evidence which you give before the coroner

Answer - It is I think

JOHN B. LAW

(The following is a true copy of the paper referred to in the last question above), to wit:

The evidence of John B. Law, taken on the 27th February, 1860, pursuant to adjournment, in the counting-room of Washington Dickinson, in Franklin *county*, Virginia deposes and says:

That he was at the counting-room of Washington Dickinson, on Saturday, the 25th February, 1860, and saw James Clement present a pistol he did not know at whom and at that moment he turned away and heard a report of a pistol immediately, and thinks it was the report of James Clement's pistol and thinks, also, that it was the first one fired. He, also, saw John Anthony Smith come out of the counting-room with a pistol in one hand and a bowie-knife in the other, soon after the firing ceased and that the knife and hand of said Smith was bloody

J.B. LAW

The witness admits that this is a true copy of the testimony given by him before the coroner's inquest.

BENJAMIN F. COOPER, J.P.

DEPOSITION OF JAMES M. GIBSON

James M. Gibson being called and sworn, says:

Question by counsel for *defence* - State whether you had any conversation with James, Ralph or William Clement in relation to any difficulty they expected to have with the defendants or either of them

Answer - I had a conversation Saturday, in the early part of the day, with James Clement. I was out there in the end of the porch at the store. I spoke to James Clement. "The taking of the depositions was a slow business." He said, "yes". I spoke of going home and he said it wasn't *worth while* to be in a hurry that they would settle the hash after a while probably. That is all the conversation I had with him

Question - State whether or not, at any previous time, you had any conversation with any of the said Clements about any difficulty they expected to have with the said defendants, or either of them

Answer - I have talked with James Clement several times since that scrape they had at Sandy Level. I don't know that he said that he expected to have any difficulty. I recollect having a conversation with him at Muse's he was saying to me there that I had understood he *reconed* how bad they had treated him that old Vincent Witcher was the evil of it and he wished he might die before it was settled that it might save him the trouble of killing him

Question - When did you have that conversation

Answer - It was after that scrape at Sandy Level. I think upwards of four months ago

CROSS EXAMINED

Question by counsel for *commonwealth* - Was the conversation you allude to is the end of the porch the day of the killing

Answer - Yes

Question - Who was present

Answer - I don't know who was present or that any one was exactly present

Question - In the conversations that you alluded to have you not heard him say that he only intended to defend himself if he was attacked

Answer - No. I never heard him say that that I recollect of

Question - In the conversation which he spoke of Capt. Witcher as the evil of his bad treatment did he say that he would kill Capt. Witcher or any of his party if they would let him alone

Answer - No. However said that he would kill any of them

Question - Did you have more than one conversation with James Clement on the day of the difficulty upon the subject of the difficulty

Answer - No, I did not

EXAMINATION IN CHIEF RESUMED

Question by counsel for *defence* - In your reply to the question before the last, did you not mean to state that you never heard James Clement say that he would kill any of them if they would let him alone

Answer - I did. He never said that he would kill any of them

Question - Did you hear James Clement say that he would kill Capt. Witcher or any of his party unless they would let him alone

Answer - No. I never heard him say that he would kill any of them

JAMES M. GIBSON

DEPOSITION OF SILAS W. EVANS

Silas W. Evans, being called and sworn, says:

Question by counsel for *defence* - State if you had any conversation with any of the deceased parties about the difficulty apprehended with the defendants or say of them, if you had, state it

Answer - I had a conversation with James Clement on Friday before the occurrence took place on Saturday. I was standing in the door. He came out by me and *sorter* touched me on the arm and I followed him out, and he asked me if I thought that the *Witcher's* would break him up yet. I told him that I didn't know whether they would or not, but if I had heard the truth that I thought that they ought to break his neck. And he asked me then if I had heard both tales, and I told him nothing more than *rumurs* in the neighborhood, and he said he thought so too if they be true reports, or if the reports were true. I remarked then that I was going home. He told me not to leave, that the fun hadn't commenced yet. I told him that such fun as they generally had didn't suit me and he told me that I wouldn't be hurt - not to be afraid. I stepped back to the door and nodded my head to Mr. James Rice. He came out and I told him to lets go home and he said that we would go home. He started home and Mr. Clement was walking backwards and forwards in the porch-floor, and he remarked again not to leave, that the fun hadn't commenced yet. I remarked to him again that that was a kind of fun that I didn't want to see, and I told him that from what I heard that they were bad marksmen that they generally shot too low. He, Mr. Clement, remarked that from what they told him, that he took pretty good aim at his man over yonder that he struck him somewhere about here, putting his hand somewhere near about the groin, and the ball struck a money purse or *port-monie*, I don't recollect which, and ranged around towards his hip. Mr. Shack Law was standing there at the time and then him and Mr. Clement went off together and went into what I call a private conversation as there was no person about there and me and Mr. Rice went off home

Question - What time of day was this

Answer - I think it was between one and three o'clock

Question - Was any witness then under examination

Answer - I think there was a lady then giving her deposition. Miss or Mrs. Shelton, I think

Question - Did you return the next day

Answer - No, I did not

CROSS EXAMINATION

Question by counsel for *commonwealth* - How many conversations with James Clement, on Friday before the killing, did you have

Answer - Two

Question - Did you not observe some persons standing near you in one of the conversations

Answer - I did

Question - Did not James Clement say that he would shoot back at any of them if they shot at him, or *some thing* to that amount

Answer - I don''t recollect hearing James Clement''s making any such remark

Question - How long were you engaged in conversation with James Clement that day

Answer - I couldn''t exactly state how long. I don''t suppose from the first to the last, that we were in conversation more than fifteen or twenty minutes. Not more than a half hour at the extent because I was fearful to be about there

Question - Didn''t you apprehend as much danger from side as the other

Answer - I did not, because I had never seen or heard anything like from the Witchers

Question - You spoke of seeing some persons present during the conversation alluded to, who were they

Answer - James Rice was one of the men, and Shack Law was another one, and if there was any more, I have no recollection of who they were

Question - Were you and James Clement of very friendly terms

Answer - We was, as far as I know

Question - Did he receive your remark about breaking his neck, in a very friendly way

Answer - He did - he laughed

Question - When he was speaking of not seeing the fun yet, was he not apparently in a good humor

Answer - I *don'* know when he spoke of them his countenance somewhat changed he spoke tolerably short his face turned a little red

Question - Did you tell Captain Witcher, or any of his party of this conversation, of James Clement''s manner and the change of his countenance before the fight

Answer - I did not no other person

Question - How did the prisoners find out since that you knew these facts

Answer - Saturday at Dickinson"s store I was talking to Wash Dickinson. I think there was some other person lying around, and I made remarks about James Clement inviting me to stay and see the fun. There was a man remarked to me that I would be summoned. I don"t know whether that man told them or who, but I got a message that *Doct.* Poindexter wanted to see me. He, *Doct.* Poindexter asked me what remarks James Clement had made about the fun, and I told him

Question - When James Clement made these remarks about the fun not being over, had the deposition of Betsy Bennett then been taken
Answer - I don"t know

EXAMINATION IN CHIEF RESUMED

Question by counsel for *defence* - Was Shack Law and Rice directly present, so that they could hear the above conversation

Answer - They heard the last conversation the first they did not

SILAS W. EVANS

DEPOSITION OF WILLIAM G. POINDEXTER

William G. Poindexter, being called and sworn on behalf of the *commonwealth*, says:

Question by counsel for *commonwealth* - Were you at Brooks" on Saturday after the combat had occurred

Answer - I was

Question - Did you carry away from here any weapons belonging to any of the accused, or that were given to you by was of the accused

Answer - I did

Question - State whose they were and what kind of weapons they were

Answer - Oliver Smith"s bowie-knife - no others

Question - Who *give* it to you

Answer - Oliver *give* it to me

Question - Was it bloody

Answer - No, it was not

       W.G. POINDEXTER

DEPOSITION OF ROBERT M. MITCHELL

Robert M. Mitchell, being called again for commonwealth

Question -Do you recollect the position of your chair when you arose to administer the oath to Betsy Bennett

Answer - I think my chair was *setting* with the back against the jam when I arose.

Question - Was there room behind your chair, between that and the jam, for a man to stand

Answer - I don"t suppose there was, unless the chair had been moved.

Question - Did you observe anybody standing between the chair and jam after you went back to resume the taking of the depositions

Answer - I did not

Question - Was there anybody standing between the chair and jam after you went back to resume the taking of the depositions

Answer - I did not

Question - Was there *any body* on the left of your chair as you sat in it between that and the desk

Answer - I think not there was not room for them, I don"t think

CROSS EXAMINATION

Question by counsel for *defence* - By the jam do you mean the wall back of you

Answer - I mean part of the house and part of the fire-place

Question - In summing up the oath was your mind so profoundly *abstracted* in studying it as to call off your attention from surrounding objects

Answer - I think it was

EXAMINATION IN CHIEF

Question by counsel for *commonwealth* - Was your mind so much engaged that you do not know where you *was* sitting

Answer - No it was not.

ROBERT MITCHELL

Question by counsel for *commonwealth* - State whether or not you were present when George Finney came down to Mrs. Ralph Clements to bring her up to her mother's on the evening of the killing

Answer - I was

Question - State how long George Finney remained there that evening

Answer - I can't be positive what space of time he remained there not more than a half hour it mightn't have been that long

Question - Did you see him when he came and when he went away

Answer - I did

Question - State whether or not you were in the room with him all the time he was there

Answer - I can't be positive whether I was or not, but I was in -- {sic} room part of the time

Question - Where were you when you were not in the room

Answer - I was up stairs and in the other room

Question - When you were up stairs who was up there with you

Answer - Mrs. Clement and my sister, Elizabeth Bennett

Question - When you were in the other room who was in there

Answer - Part of the time by myself, and Mrs. Clement part of the time

Question - Where was Miss Bennett when you were in the other room

Answer - I can't be positive where she was she was passing about there

Question - Was she engaged in preparing to fix Mrs. Clement off, or any other business

Answer - She was helping her to dress and helping her to get her child's clothing

Question - Did you see or hear any conversation between Elizabeth Bennett and George Finney during his stay at Mrs. Clements

Answer - I didn't

Question - Did George Finney have any conversation with you about the killing

Answer - He did. I asked him if he knew how the fuss commenced, and he said that he did not, that he *ware* not present at the time he said he was started home, and he heard the *relarm* and he turned back again he said he asked who commenced it, and he said that James Clement was in the act of shooting his grandfather, and he shot and *stabed* him first. He then asked me if I knew who commenced it, and I told him I did not know anything about it. I was not present

Question - Where about the house did this did this conversation take place

Answer - In the passage at the door on the right hand side as you go in at the door

Question - How were you standing towards each other fronting, or side-ways, or how

Answer - *Sorter* side-ways to his right arm

Question - Do you recollect how you were dressed that day

Answer - Very well. A striped cotton dress, I had on a red checked calico bonnet

CROSS EXAMINATION

Question by counsel for *defence* - How was Betsy Bennett dressed at the time

Answer - I don''t recollect

Question - Has not she a striped dress and red bonnet

Answer - Yes

Question - Did she wear them to the store that day

Answer - I don''t recollect

Question - Did Betsy Bennett give you any account of the fight at that time

Answer - I heard her speaking some little about it

Question - Was George Finney present

Answer - Not when I heard her speaking about it he wasn''t

Question - Did you see Betsy Bennett and George Finney standing together in the door, no other person being immediately near

Answer - I did not

Question - Where did Betsy Bennett stay during the giving of the deposition

Answer - She *staid* the night at my house

Question - Are you the wife of the overseer of Ralph Clement deceased

Answer - I am

Question - State whether or not Ralph Clement or James or William were firing *there* pistols off a good deal some time before this killing

Answer - If they did I did not hear them

Question - Was Betsy Bennett with you

Answer - Yes

GILLY ANN HUFFMAN

DEPOSITION OF JOHN C. LAW

John C. Law, being called and sworn, says:

Question by counsel for *commonwealth* - State anything that John B. Law may have said to you and Johnson Clement about the position of James Clement, when the firing began

Answer - In the first place, he said that Vincent Witcher arose up, placed his hand to his bosom he took a fright and left, seeing that there was a fight to take place. I asked him then if he knew who shot the first pistol he said while running he saw the hand of James Clement and John Anthony Smith reaching for one another and the smoke arising from the hand of James Clement

Question - Did John B. Law tell you that James Clement was on the floor at the feet of the bed when he last saw him

Answer - The way he expressed himself was this that James Clement was down on the floor at the foot of the bed at the time he saw his and John A. Smith reaching for one another

Question - Where did John B. Law say he was going when he saw James Clement and John A. Smith reaching at each other

Answer - My understanding was that his allusion was that he was getting out of the way

Question - Did John B. Law ever tell you that some other person told him that James Clement was at the foot of the bed

Answer - He did not

Question - Did you hear a conversation between Silas W. Evans and James Clement on the Friday before the killing, in which Clement asked Evans to stay and see the fun Can you state why Clement said so

Answer - Wash, Evans, George Sampson, James Rice and myself were together on Friday evening at the end of the porch at Dickinson"s, and in a conversation, James Clement came out and spoke to me and joined us in the conversation. Wash, Evans, I think, remarked that he was going home or wanted to go home. James says, "oh no, hold on and see the fun", which caused me to take notice of him, James Clement. Which from that conversation led to the conversation between Wash, Evans, and I couldn"t say whether James Rice joined in it, though he was present and heard it, in relation to shooting and as to the precise words I am not sure that I could give the precise words, but I think that Wash, Evans remarked to him that he "didn"t wish to join in such fun as this", for he generally shot too low. By some remarks I made to James Clement I drew him off from the crowd. He walked to me and threw his arm around my shoulder. We started off down the lane together in the direction of Mr. Finney"s

CROSS EXAMINATION

Question by counsel for *defence* - When did you have the above conversation with John B. Law

Answer - I can't say what evening of last week

Question - Where was it

Answer - We were in the hollow just beyond the store where there was some logs by the side of the fence

Question - Who was along besides yourself and John B. Law

Answer - Johnson Clement was the only other man that was along

Question - How long have you attended on this case as a witness

Answer - I was summoned here last Wednesday

Question - At whose instance

Answer - By the commonwealth, according to my subpoena.

Question - Was John B. Law then summoned as a witness

Answer - I don't know

Question - In the conversation aforesaid, did John B. Law mention the fact of any friend having given him information on the subject, what {do} you say he was talking about

Answer - No, he did not

Question - Did you not state to Robert Powell and Waller Wright, that from a remark you heard James Clement make on Friday evening before the *rencounter*, that you were afraid a difficulty would ensue, and that you advised him not to have one

Answer - I did, before Robert Powell and Waller Wright

Question - State whether or not you have had any agency whatever on conversing with people with a view of having them summoned against these defendants

Answer - I have not

Question - Were you a witness before the coroner's inquest

Answer - I was not a witness but on the coroner's inquest - one of them

Question - Was the above conversation with John B. Law before or after the inquest

Answer - I think it was after the inquest

Question - Had you any conversation with the said John B. Law on the said subject since the one above, mentioned in the hollow

Answer - I think that I have

Question - Did you not state in the presence of Robert Powell and Charles Powell, or one of them, that in a conversation between you and John B. Law, the said John B. Law gave substantially the same account of the first firing that Robert Powell did before the inquest

Answer - I did not say substantially, as I recollect, but did say parallel

Question - Did you know what you were summoned for in this case shortly after you *was* summoned

Answer - I did not, and frequently said to people I didn't know what they had me summoned for, that I know nothing myself, that I had only heard people talk

EXAMINATION IN CHIEF

Question by counsel for *commonwealth* - You speak of a conversation with Robert N. Powell, in which you told him that you heard James Clement make a remark that induced you to fear a *reencounter*. What was the remark

Answer - I said to him, "Jim, why do you make such remark as this" Says he, "they are preparing for something." Says I, "Jim, as I have always told you before, you are too excitable, and you are excited now." He said, "Jack, they are going to kill me." Says I, "Jim, what in the world do you mean by making such remarks as that" Says he, "I saw Mr. Dabney give Sile Dudley two pistols." Says I, "Jim, *its* all humbuggery and you be cool and deliberate and have no fighting." Says he, "Jack, you have always given me good advice and I will take it, and so as I have always done, and I will not be the aggressor, but the defender, and if I am shot at, I'll be damned if I don't shoot the man that shoots at me." Says I, "Jim, if all of them will act the way that you have promised to act, there will be no fighting". Right there we parted

Question - In what relation does Silas Dudley stand to Capt. Witcher

Answer - There is no blood relation that I know of. I have been told that Silas Dudley married his grand-daughter, a sister of James Clement's wife

Question - In the conversation you had with Robert Powell, with reference to John B. Law's statements did you not allude to his statement before the coroner

Answer - I never heard John B. Law''s statement before the coroner, but according to his statement (Robert Powell''s) before the jury, and what John B. Law had told me in relation to the first fire, it was parallel

Question - Had you conversed such with John upon this subject

Answer - As I have stated before, me and John B. Law *has* talked about it at different times

JOHN C. LAW

Adjourned till to-morrow morning at 9 o''clock.

BENJAMIN F. COOPER, J.P.

DEPOSITION OF WILLIAM H. HUTCHERSON

William H. Hutcherson being called and sworn for *defence* says

I was in the counting room at Dickinson"s on the 25th last month. There was about two shots fired before I got to the door, and one about the time I got in the door leading to the store-room. I got out as quick as I could. I heard the firing. I *recon* all of it don"t know who fired I went back after the firing ceased I saw two men lying on the floor dead, and two or more men hold of one wounded. I was told that it was William and James Clement. I knew that it was Ralph that the men was in the act of raising when I went in they put him on the bed. I think that Mr. Mackenheimer, and I know that Dr. Baker was one of the men that assisted to raise him Mr. Carter too was in

Question by counsel for *defence* - Were you present at the angry words that parsed between Vincent Witcher and Ralph Clement

Answer - Yes, I was

Question - Where were you

Answer - I was sitting on a kind of desk that sets under the stair-steps

Question - State the words and what the parties did while speaking them

Answer - Ralph Clement gave Capt. Witcher the lie or damned lie, I disremember which. They were sitting in their chairs when Ralph Clement spoke those words. Capt. Witcher, before Ralph Clement gave him the lie, was talking to Squire Mitchell, saying something in regard to a female witness which they had there. Capt. Witcher told Squire Mitchell that they had brought her there or something to that amount. Ralph Clement then said that anybody said that told a lie or damned lie, I disremember which. Capt. Witcher, after a few minutes, pointed to Ralph Clement, looked that way, seemed to be talking to Ralph Clement. He said, "Mr. Clement, you must make your remarks more definite". I think was the words. He, Capt. Witcher, arose from his seat about that time, and about that time I heard the report of a pistol

Question - When did Ralph Clement rise

Answer - He arose or partly arose immediately after he gave Capt. Witcher the lie

Question - Did he sit down again

Answer - I don"t recollect seeing him *set* down any more

Question - While *their* rising what did he do

Answer - He put his hand on his breast, I thought seemed to be unbuttoning his vest, his hand about the buttons seemed to be working there

187

Question - How many of his hands did he use

Answer - He only had one on his vest the other was on the table I thought

Question - Did Vincent Witcher attempt to draw a pistol

Answer - When he got up out of his chair he turned his fact to the fire-place, and seemed to be I thought, in the act of drawing weapons. He had his right hand before him I thought about his breast

Question - When you heard the first pistol what direction were you looking

Answer - I think I was looking at Capt. Witcher, but am not positive

Question - Had the pistol fired while you were glancing at Ralph Clement, Vincent Witcher from your position, would you not necessarily have seen whether either of them fired it

Answer - I think I should, unless Capt. Witcher had fired right before him or with his left hand. I was rather on his right. I could see his right arm

Question - Who fired the first pistol

Answer - I do not know

Question - What induced you to leave the room

Answer - The firing

Question - From what quarter did the firing come

Answer - I thought the first report was from about the bed

Question - Did you start to leave on the report of the first pistol

Answer - Yes

Question - State whether that report came from the direction that might be expected if Vincent Witcher fired it

Answer - I think not

Question - When you left the room were you not apprehensive, from the report of the first pistol, that there was danger of being shot from another direction than from the position which Vincent Witcher occupied

Answer - Yes. I was

Question - Have you any impression that Ralph Clement used the damned lie

Answer - Yes I rather have

Question - What reply did Ralph Clement make if any, to Vincent Witcher when he said "Make your charge more direct"

Answer - None at all that I heard

Question - Did you see Addison Witcher

Answer - I saw him before the firing commenced

Question - Where was he and what was he doing

Answer - He walked into the counting-room to about the middle of the floor, and spoke to Samuel C. Mattox. He was smoking his pipe

Question - Did you observe him during the quarreling If so, where was he

Answer - I did not observe him

EXAMINATION

Question by counsel for *commonwealth* - When were you summoned in this case

Answer - On yesterday evening, late

Question - Who summoned you

Answer - Mr. Snead Adams

Question - To whom had you communicated the facts you have dictated here to-day before you were summoned

Answer - I talked to several. I didn't mention it to any of the prisoners. I talked - - {sic} Abram Hancock for one and to John C. Hutcherson for another

Question - Was the shot you say was fired about the time you got in the door fired as you were in the door going out

Answer - Yes, when I was in or about the door

Question - Which door

Answer - The door leading from the counting-room into the store-room

Question - Was not the crowd rushing out when you heard this shot

Answer - It was from the --- {sic} firing commenced

Question - Do you know whether John C. Hutcherson got out of the room before or after you did

Answer - He was just before me I think

Question - Are you certain that this was the second shot

Answer - I think it was the third

Question - Did you discover any intermission after the first shot

Answer - A short intermission after the first shot

Question - Were you very deliberate

Answer - Not very

Question - Were any persons between you while you were *setting* and Ralph Clement

Answer - There was not. I saw Ralph Clement while he was speaking. I saw him before he gave Capt. Witcher the lie too

Question. - Was any person between yourself and Capt. Witcher

Answer - There was not immediately I could see him when he was talking to Squire Mitchell and I saw him when he got up out of his chair

Question - Were there many persons in the room

Answer - A good many

Question - Did you see John M. Hutcherson in the room

Answer - I don''t recollect that I did

Question. - Were you not *setting* on the desk at the back of Ralph Clement

Answer - *Setting* rather to his left

Question - What was Capt. Witcher''s relative position to you

Answer - When he was *setting* in the chair I was rather to his right

Question - When Ralph Clement and Vincent Witcher each arose, did they not front one another

Answer - They did

Question - When they were fronting each other was not Ralph Clement"s back to you

Answer - I was to Ralph Clement"s left

Question - Did you see his front and his right hand distinctly

Answer - I did

Question - Can you explain how it is that you can see distinctly a man"s front and right hand when his left side is presented to you

Answer - Yes when Ralph Clement first got up he seemed to be restless and turned to the left keeping his face towards the table looking towards Capt. Witcher

Question – Did you notice his face particularly

Answer – I did

Question - Did you notice his person very particularly

Answer - Not very

Question - Did you see his vest button

Answer - I don"t know that I did

Question - Was the expression of his face at the time you saw his hand upon the table angry and defiant

Answer - He looked about as usual to me

Question - Do you recollect the words that Capt. Witcher used, to which Clement gave the lie

Answer - I don"t recollect the identical words

Question - Give the identical words as near as you can

Answer - Capt. Witcher was speaking to Mr. Mitchell. He said "they had brought her there or had her brought there" as well as I recollect

Question - Was that all Capt. Witcher said upon the subject

Answer - That is all I recollect hearing him say

Question - Did Capt. Witcher not say that he heard they had brought her there

Answer - It might have been his words, but I don't recollect hearing him say that

Question - When Capt. Witcher arose fronting to Mr. Ralph Clement, was not his manner very angry

Answer - It seemed to be somewhat angry

Question - What did he point at Clement

Answer - His hand

Question - Was that while he was standing or *setting*

Answer - About the time he was in the act of rising I think

Question - Was Mr. Ralph Clement up then

Answer - I think he was I think they were both rising about the same time

Question - When you saw them rising in the act as you suppose of drawing arms did you not immediately leave the room

Answer - As well as I recollect I got down off the desk about that time but did not immediately start to leave the room

Question - When you got off the desk how far were you from Ralph Clement

Answer - I was about six or eight feet I recon I couldn't tell exactly

Question by same – How far from a straight line drawn from yourself to Capt. Witcher would Ralph Clement have been?

Answer – I *recon* it would have – {sic{ five or six feet but don't know exactly

Question - If a rapid firing had taken place between Witcher and Ralph Clement would you not have been in some danger

Answer - I would not

Question - Would you be willing to stand where you was standing after you got off the desk, if there had been a fight going on with pistols between two men occupying the relative position of Witcher and Clement

Answer - No, I would not

Question - Did not the crowd begin to leave immediately upon the rising of Mr. Witcher and Mr. Clement

Answer - They began to fall back from towards the fire-place and make towards the door rather
Question - Did you see anybody on the bed at the time these gentlemen arose

Answer - I did not

Question - How far was Capt. Witcher from the bed

Answer - When he was standing I would suppose three or four feet

Question - Your observations of many things seem to have been minute. Did you notice the bed

Answer - I did before the *fracus* began but not afterwards

Question - How long before the *fracus* began did you notice the bed

Answer - I *recon* it was some ten or fifteen minutes probably

Question - Do you not know at that time that there was certainly three or more persons on the bed

Answer - I do not

Question - Who *were* on it

Answer - I saw James Clement lying on the bed I didn"t notice anybody else

Question - How was his position on the bed

Answer - He was lying lengthways on his back

Question - How far was he from where Capt. Witcher was *setting*

Answer - Two or three feet probably not more than two feet

Question - Was not Capt. Witcher when he arose immediately between James Clement and the corner of the desk by the fire-place near the back of the magistrate"s chair

Answer - Capt. Witcher was between James Clement"s head and where I saw him lying before that on the bed and the desk by the fire-place

Question - From where you were when you started to leave the room did you not have to go in the direction of the bed, and near to the foot of it

Answer - I did

Question - Then if the first shot had been from the bed, why could you not have seen the smoke

Answer - I was glancing at Capt. Witcher and Ralph Clement I was not looking toward the bed

Question - Do you state that you were glancing at Witcher and Clement while you were leaving the room

Answer - When I started out I kept my head towards the door

Question - You stated that you were not afraid of being shot by Vincent Witcher, but you were nevertheless afraid of being shot if you remained in the house. What did you see from anybody else to cause you to fear being shot

Answer - I saw nothing

Question - How long before the firing was it that you last saw Addison Witcher

Answer - I don"t recollect how long it was, but I would suppose from a quarter to a half hour

Question - Did you see William Clement do or say anything to provoke anybody during the whole time of taking of those depositions

Answer - I don"t recollect of ever having seen him before. I saw him lying dead

The witness here wishes to state that in making his statement about the position of James Clement whilst lying on the bed he made a mistake in saying that he was lying on his back. He was lying on his side with his face towards the witness with his elbow on the bed and his head or face resting on his hand.

WM. H. HUTCHERSON

DEPOSITION OF ALFRED L. H. MUSE

Alfred L.H. Muse, being called and sworn on the part of the *defence*, says:

Question by counsel for *defence* - Were you at Dickinson''s store at the taking of the depositions in the suit of Clement''s by etc. against Clement

Answer - I was there on Thursday the day of the commencement

Question - State whether or not you saw any rude conduct on the part of James Clement towards Vincent Witcher If you did, state what it was

Answer - I thought I did Capt. Witcher was in the porch I saw James Clement pass by him and rubbed *agin* him and knocked his pipe out of his pocket I *mought* have been mistaken, but I thought he did it a purpose

Question - At the time he knocked the pipe out of his pocket was there, or was there not sufficient - -- for his passing without doing so

Answer - I thought there was

Question - State whether or not Vincent Witcher resented it

Answer - He did not that I saw he stooped down picked up his pipe walked off to the lower end of the porch the last I noticed of it

Question - State whether or not Vincent Witcher was conduction or superintending the taking of the testimony for the plaintiff on that day

Answer - I do not know. I saw Capt. Witcher whispering to Mr. Dabney

Question - Was not Vincent Witcher present all the time said depositions was taking and did you see counsel put any question immediately upon conversing with Vincent Witcher

Answer - He was present a great portion of the time, on Thursday while I was there and I was there all day. I saw him - {Note: the transcribed copy in the library ends here and does not contain the rest of the information that follows} frequently conversing with his counsel Mr Dabney. Mr. Dabney would *ax* questions

Question by same – During your stay did you not see any abrupt conduct respecting the depositions between James and Ralph Clement?

Answer – Yes I saw them fall out and saw Mr Ralph Clement get up and say to James Clement if he didn''t hush his mouth go and sit down and let him alone that he would quit and go home.

CROSS EXAMINATION

Question by counsel for *commonwealth* - Has Capt Witcher the reputation of being a brave and spirited man

Answer – I think he has

Question by same – Is it likely from Capt Witchers character or spirit that he would allow any man wantonly to insult him without resenting it

Answer – I don"t think he would

Question by same – Have you not heretofore had a difficulty with Mr Ralph A Clement

Answer – Yes we had a difficulty. Mr Clement forced that difficulty on me whether I would or not. I tried to beg out I got up and left twice during the investigation of this matter and finally disputed my word the third time. I had stood it just as long as I could stand it and remarked to him that he had disputed my word the third time and he shouldn"t do it any more. He gathered a chair {and} struck at me. I caught the chair jerked it away from him gathered him by the head. He never whipped me. We afterwards made friends and my *feeling* were perfectly good towards him to the day of his death.

Question by same – Are you *rellated* or connected to the Witchers
Answer - There is no blood relations that I know of Capt Witchers brother Jim married my wife"s cousin- first cousin.

EXAMINATION IN CHIEF RESUMED

Question by counsel for *defence* - State if you are acquainted with the general character of Samuel Swanson for amiability and quietness. If so state what it is

Answer – I am I think he is generally looked upon as being as quiet and as peaceable as any man in the *county* of Pittsylvania

A.L.H. Muse

DEPOSITION OF JOSIAH F. POWELL

Question - State if you ever had any conversation with James Clement during the taking of the depositions in relation to any difficulty with Vincent Witcher or any of his family which he expected to have during the taking of the depositions

Answer – I had some with him Friday morning and he said he expected the Witchers would fight Thursday but they appeared to be cool as cucumbers I think that is about all he said

Question – Were you present when James Clement started off to attend to taking depositions from home

Answer - Yes I was

Question - State whether he armed himself

Answer- Yes he did

Question by same - State if he said anything – {sic} in arguing with himself If he did – {sic}

Answer – He didn't say anything

JOSIAH F. POWELL

A copy – Teste
        A.J. NAFF
        Deputy for RO . A. SCOTT,
        Clerk of Franklin County Court

DECISION OF EXAMINING JUSTICE

The following was the written decision of the Justice who committed Capt. Witcher and his jparth:

"GENTLEMEN PRISONERS – Listen to my decision. I have listened to the evidence of this cause with a perfect impartiality if I know my own heart. I have listened to the able and manly argument of the cause. I have regretted that the duty which I feel bound to discharge is a painful one. A most fearful deed has been committed among us. Do we live in a country of law? Then, if we do, this matter, so grave in all its relations, demands a further legal investigation and I would not deserve the name of a man of justice, if, with my views of the law, I should discharge the accused. They must all go on to further trial. I must yet go a little further. I cannot say that only a light suspicion of guilt falls upon them. I wish I could do so. The Constable is required, therefore, to take them all to jail and he must summon a sufficient guard for that purpose.

Gentlemen, on all sides, I will not hear any more. Constable, look to the prisoners, for you are responsible."

CLERK'S CERTIFICATE

Franklin County Clerk"s Office, May16th, 1860:
I, Robert A. Scott, Clerk of the County Court in and for the County of Franklin, in the State of Virginia, do certify that Dr. Richard M. Taliaferro, Robert Bush, Moses C. Greer, Isaac Cannaday and Jonathan H. McNeil, Esqrs., composed the Court for the examination of Vincent Witcher, Addison Witcher, John A. Smith, Vincent O. Smith, James R. Clement and William C. Clement. I further certify, that I have been informed (not knowing the fact myself, and the records not showing the fact) that Isaac Cannaday and Jonathan McNeil, Esqrs., were, upon the examination of the above named Vincent Witcher and others, for the said offence, in favor of sending the said prisoners on to the Circuit Court for further trial, but were overruled by the other three Justices composing the Court.
     Given under my hand, the day and date above written.
          RO. A. SCOTT, Clerk

CHANCERY COURT ORDER BOOK #11, Pages 520 thru 524, 527
and Book #12, Page 45

Thursday morning, March 8th 1860. Court met pursuant to adjournment same justice as on yesterday.

Franklin County Chancery Court Order Book 11, Page 520

At a Court held for Franklin County at the Courthouse on the 15th day of March 1860 for the examination of Vincent Witcher, John A. Smith, Vincent O. Smith, Samuel Swanson and Addison Witcher charged with three separate felonies by them committed in this, that they did on the 25th day of February 1860 in the Counting room of Dickinson"s Store in said County, *Wilfully*, deliberately and with premeditation murder and kill Ralph A. Clement, James R. Clement & William C. Clement.

Present Richard M. Taliaferro, Robert Bush, Moses C. Greer, Jonathan H. McNiel and Isaac Cannaday Gent Justices.

William H. Cook Esqr licensed to practice law in the Courts of this Commonwealth who took the several oaths required by law is admitted to practice in this Court.

The said Vincent Witcher, John A. Smith, Vincent O. Smith, Samuel Swanson and Addison Witcher were led to the Bar in custody of the Jailor of this Court. And on the motion of the Attorney for the Commonwealth and for reasons appearing to the Court the examination is adjourned till tomorrow. And on the further motion of the Attorney for the Commonwealth it is ordered that Washington Dickinson, John C. Law and James Kemp be summoned to appear here on the 16" of this month at 10 o"clock to show cause if any they can why attachment should not be issued against them for their contempt in failing to appear her *to day* as witnesses on behalf of the Commonwealth against the said Vincent Witcher & others. And the said Vincent Witcher, John A. Smith, Vincent O. Smith, Samuel Swanson and Addison Witcher are remanded to Jail.

And the attorney for the Commonwealth & the prisoners in proper person in open Court consenting that this Court shall examine & determine each of the three charges at the same time.

Ordered that Court be adjourned till tomorrow morning at 10 O Clock.
     R.M. Taliaferro

Chancery Court Order Book 11, Page 521

At a Court continued and held for Franklin County at the Courthouse on the 16" day of March 1860 for the examination of Vincent Witcher, John A. Smith, Vincent O. Smith, Samuel Swanson and Addison Witcher charged with the felonies aforesaid by them committed in this, that they did on the 25" day of February 1860 in the Counting room of Dickinson"s Store in said

County, *wilfully*, deliberately and with premeditation murder and kill Ralph A. Clement, James R. Clement and William C. Clement.

Present Richard M. Taliaferro, Robert Bush, Moses C. Greer, Jonathan H. McNiel and Isaac Cannaday – Gent. Justices

James Garland Esqr licensed to practice law in the Courts of this Commonwealth, who took the several oaths required by law is admitted to practice in this Court.

The said Vincent Witcher, John A. Smith, Vincent O. Smith, Samuel Swanson and Addison Witcher were again led to the Bar in Custody of the Jailor of this Court. And thereupon the Court proceeded to examine divers witnesses and not being able to complete the testimony, the examination is continued till tomorrow. And the said prisoners were removed to Jail.

Ordered that Court be adjourned till tomorrow morning at 9 O'clock.

> R.M. Taliaferro

At a Court continued and held for Franklin County at the Courthouse on the 17" day of March 1860 for the examination of Vincent Witcher, John A. Smith, Vincent O. Smith, Samuel Swanson and Addison Witcher charged with three felonies aforesaid by them committed in this, that they did on the 25" day of February 1860 in the Counting room of Dickinson"s Store in said County *wilfully*, deliberately and with premeditation murder and kill Ralph A. Clement , James R. Clement and William C. Clement.

Present Richard M. Taliaferro, Robert Bush, Moses C. Greer, Jonathan H. McNiel and Isaac Cannaday – Gent Justices

The said Vincent Witcher, John A. Smith, Vincent O. Smith, Samuel Swanson and Addison Witcher were again led to the Bar in custody of the Jailor of this Court. And thereupon the Court again proceeded to the examination of divers witnesses and not being able to complete the examination the same is adjourned until Monday next.

And the said prisoners are remanded to jail.

Ordered that Court be adjourned till Monday morning 10 O'clock

> R.M. Taliaferro

Chancery Court Order Book 11, Page 522

At a Court continued and held for Franklin County at the Courthouse on the 19th day of March 1860 for the examination of Vincent Witcher, John A. Smith, Vincent O. Smith, Samuel Swanson and Addison Witcher charged with the felonies aforesaid by them committed in this, that they did on the 25" day of February 1860 in the Counting room of Dickinson"s Store in said

County *wilfully*, deliberately and with premeditation murder and kill Ralph A. Clement, James R. Clement and William C. Clement.

Present Richard M. Taliaferro, Robert Bush, Moses C. Greer, Jonathan H. McNiel and Isaac Cannaday – Gent Justices

The said Vincent Witcher, John A. Smith, Vincent O. Smith, Samuel Swanson and Addison Witcher were again led to the Bar in custody of the Jailor of this Court.   And the Court again proceeded to the examination of divers witnesses and not being able to complete the examination the same is adjourned till tomorrow.

And the prisoners are remanded to Jail.

Ordered that Court be adjourned till tomorrow morning 9 O'Clock.

      R.M. Taliaferro

At a Court continued and held for Franklin County at the Courthouse on the 20th day of March 1860 for the examination of Vincent Witcher, John A. Smith, Vincent O. Smith, Samuel Swanson and Addison Witcher charged with the felonies aforesaid by them committed in this, that they did on the 25" day of February 1860 in the Counting room of Dickinson"s Store in said County *wilfully*, deliberately and with premeditation murder and kill Ralph A. Clement, James R. Clement and William C. Clement.

Present Richard M. Taliaferro, Robert Bush, Moses C. Greer, Jonathan H. McNiel and Isaac Cannaday – Gent Justices

The said Vincent Witcher, John A. Smith, Vincent O. Smith, Samuel Swanson and Addison Witcher were again led to the Bar in custody of the Jailor of this Court.   And the Court again proceeded to the examination of divers witnesses and not being able to complete the examination the same is adjourned till tomorrow.

And the prisoners are remanded to Jail.

Ordered that Court be adjourned till tomorrow morning 9 *O'Clock*.

      R.M. Taliaferro

Chancery Court Book 11, Page 523

At a Court continued and held for Franklin County at the Courthouse on the 21" day of March 1860 for the examination of Vincent Witcher, John A. Smith, Vincent O. Smith, Samuel Swanson and Addison Witcher charged with the felonies aforesaid by them committed in this, that they did on the 25" day of February 1860 in the Counting room of Dickinson"s Store in said County *wilfully*, deliberately and with premeditation murder and kill Ralph A. Clement, James R. Clement and William C. Clement.

Present Richard M. Taliaferro, Robert Bush, Moses C. Greer, Jonathan H. McNiel and Isaac Cannaday – Gent Justices

The said Vincent Witcher, John A. Smith, Vincent O. Smith, Samuel Swanson and Addison Witcher were again led to the Bar in custody of the Jailor of this Court. And the Court again proceeded to the examination of divers witnesses and not being able to complete the examination the same is adjourned till tomorrow.

And the prisoners are remanded to Jail.

Ordered that Court be adjourned till tomorrow morning 9 O"Clock.

R.M. Taliaferro

At a Court continued and held for Franklin County at the Courthouse on the 22" day of March 1860 for the examination of Vincent Witcher, John A. Smith, Vincent O. Smith, Samuel Swanson and Addison Witcher charged with the felonies aforesaid by them committed in this, that they did on the 25" day of February 1860 in the Counting room of Dickinson"s Store in said County *wilfully*, deliberately and with premeditation murder and kill Ralph A. Clement, James R. Clement and William C. Clement.

Present Richard M. Taliaferro, Robert Bush, Moses C. Greer, Jonathan H. McNiel and Isaac Cannaday – Gent Justices

The said Vincent Witcher, John A. Smith, Vincent O. Smith, Samuel Swanson and Addison Witcher were again led to the Bar in custody of the Jailor of this Court. And the Court again proceeded to the examination of divers witnesses and not being able to complete the examination the same is adjourned till tomorrow.

And the prisoners are remanded to Jail.

Ordered that Court be adjourned till tomorrow morning 9 *O'Clock*.

R.M. Taliaferro

Chancery Court Book 11, Page 524

At a Court continued and held for Franklin County at the Courthouse on the 19th {sic} day of March 1860 for the examination of Vincent Witcher, John A. Smith, Vincent O. Smith, Samuel Swanson and Addison Witcher charged with the felonies aforesaid by them committed in this, that they did on the 25" day of February 1860 in the Counting room of Dickinson"s Store in said County *wilfully*, deliberately and with premeditation murder and kill Ralph A. Clement, James R. Clement and William C. Clement.

Present Richard M. Taliaferro, Robert Bush, Moses C. Greer, Jonathan H. McNiel and Isaac Cannaday – Gent Justices

The said Vincent Witcher, John A. Smith, Vincent O. Smith, Samuel Swanson and Addison Witcher were again led to the Bar in custody of the Jailor of this Court. And the Court having examined divers witnesses as well on behalf of the Commonwealth as of the prisoners at the Bar, who were heard in their *defence* by Counsel, is of the opinion that there is not probable cause for charging the said prisoners with the offence aforesaid, and doth order that they be *acquited* and discharged of the said offence, and go thereof without *day* .

Ordered that Court be adjourned & Since dio

       R.M. Taliaferro

       Chancery Court Book 11, Page 527

A paper purporting to be the last will and Testament of James R. Clement was produced in Court and it being proved by the oaths of James L. Rice, Edward C. Murphy and Charles J. Clement that the said paper is wholly in the hand writing of the said James R. Clement Dec.d and doth order that the said paper be admitted to record as the last will and testament of the said James R. Clement Decd. And on the motion of Charles J. Clement both will security and made oath a certificate is granted him to obtain letters of administration with the said will {can't read}.

Ordered that Amos R. Law, William V. Bernard, S.L. Walker and Samuel Smith or any three of them after being sworn for the purpose do appraise the estate of James R. Clement Decd and report according to law.

       Chancery Court Book 12, Page 45

Madison D. Carter testamentary Guardian of Lelia Maud Clement infant daughter of James R. Clement decd this day appeared in Court and executed bond and security in the amount of $6000.00 conditioned according to law.

Made in the USA
Coppell, TX
17 July 2021